D0755287

ARE YOU
RIGHT
FOR ME?

ARE YOU RIGHT FOR ME?

Seven steps to getting clarity and commitment in your relationship

ANDREW G. MARSHALL

BLOOMSBURY

LONDON · BERLIN · NEW YORK · SYDNEY

To Rosalind Lowe

Thank you for the inspiration.

First published in Great Britain 2011

Copyright © 2011 by Andrew G. Marshall

The moral right of the author has been asserted

Some of this material has appeared in a different context in
The Single Trap, which is also published by Bloomsbury.

Bloomsbury Publishing Plc
36 Soho Square,
London W1D 3QY

Bloomsbury Publishing, London, New York and Berlin

A CIP catalogue record for this book is
available from the British Library

ISBN 978 1 4088 0262 5

10 9 8 7 6 5 4 3 2 1

Typeset by Hewer Text UK Ltd, Edinburgh
Printed in Great Britain by Clays Limited, St Ives Plc

www.bloomsbury.com/andrewgmarshall

Seven steps to getting clarity and commitment in your relationship

INTRODUCTION

Seven Steps is a series of books offering straight-forward advice for creating successful and fulfilling relationships. If you've picked up this book, you are probably facing an important decision but are finding it hard to make up your mind. I am not surprised. Modern life offers a far wider range of opportunities than our parents' generation ever faced. Throw in the promise that we can be 'anything we want to be' and it's easy to become overwhelmed: trapped in the quagmire of indecision, trying to understand both our own and our partner's minds, churning over all the different options and uncertain what to do for the best.

I have two main aims in writing this book. First, to share the experiences of other people who have faced similar dilemmas, the latest research into relationships and the relevant decision-making skills. Second, to help you believe in yourself and value your own experiences. Ultimately, you are the world expert on yourself and I hope to empower you to take control of your life again.

At the centre of each of the seven steps, there is a central question. Answering these questions will help you take stock of your relationship, understand your situation better and deal with commitment issues. By the end of the book, whether you have only recently started a relationship or have been together with your partner for many years, you will be ready to move forward with confidence and without regrets.

In devising this programme, I have drawn on twenty-five years' experience working as a marital therapist. However, I have changed names, details and sometimes merged two or three of my clients' stories to protect their identity and confidentiality. In addition, I have used interviews with people not in counselling and letters written to my website. My thanks to everyone who has shared their experiences and made this book possible.

Andrew G. Marshall
www.andrewgmarshall.com

STEP 1

TAKE STOCK

In the movies, a couple meet and they just *know* that each has met that one special person. Marriage, children and eternal bliss are just a heartbeat away. Sadly, in the real world, it is much harder to work out whether a relationship has a future or not. Most of us do not have these blinding flashes or, if we've had them in the past, have been badly let down and no longer trust our own judgement.

So we hold on and hope that the longer and better we know someone, the easier it will be to make an informed choice. Unfortunately, instead of gaining clarity, we are overloaded with competing information and our mind becomes so overactive that it is almost impossible to make a good decision. If this sounds familiar, don't worry. You are not alone.

Whether you have been dating a few months (and trying to decide whether this relationship is serious) or whether you've been together for years (but your partnership has hit a wall and you're questioning the future), this book will help you understand your situation better. Instead of trying to balance all the competing pros and cons and worrying about all the possible outcomes, I will concentrate your mind on seven key questions. By the end of this journey, you will be able to face the most important question of all: *Are you right for me?*

Getting Out of Limbo

Staying up in the air, and not coming down one way or the other, is not only frustrating, but it can also do a lot of damage. Being in limbo drains energy out of your relationship, puts off dealing with the problems (which makes them seem bigger and harder to resolve than they probably are), and the general negativity destroys your self-belief.

'My boyfriend told me that I was getting only one Christmas present and it couldn't go under the tree,' said Maxine, thirty-two. 'It could mean only one thing: a proposal.' On Christmas morning, she could not get out of bed. 'I had no idea what I would reply. So I lay in bed for an hour, too frightened to come down, and mucked up the whole day.'

Maxine had been married at twenty-five but her husband was unfaithful and they were divorced after just four years. 'The first time round I didn't think twice, but now I worry that I'm a terrible judge of character. I've failed once and I couldn't cope twice.' She has been with her boyfriend for three years. 'I'm less self-conscious and, unlike with my ex-husband, who undermined my self-confidence, I feel loved for myself. What's more, I trust him implicitly. Yet when we went to a friend's wedding, I felt my fear rising just listening to them make their vows.' As it turned out, Maxine had got herself into a state for nothing. Her boyfriend did not propose and the mystery present turned out to be a portrait of her dog.

We instinctively know that stewing over a problem makes things worse, so rush straight towards the central dilemma: should I or shouldn't I commit? However, in the meantime, we ignore or take for granted much of the thinking that underpins our decision. This is why the first question for achieving clarity is:

Have you fallen for one of the unhelpful myths about relationships?

There are five common myths that could be trapping you in limbo:

1. Love at first sight

Researchers at the University of Mississippi took thirty-eight student couples, who had been on five dates, gave them a detailed questionnaire, and then repeated it four months later. They were particularly interested in the differences between the couples who continued to date and those who split up, and whether it was possible to predict which group a couple would fall into.

The results were very interesting – all the couples were unsure about whether they would keep dating. Nobody 'just knew' they were destined to be together. This is something, with the benefit of hindsight, which we retrospectively award to our relationship. The most important difference between continuing and non-continuing couples was the amount of self-disclosure at five dates. In other words, people who were more open and honest – rather than just putting on a front or being defensive – were the most romantically successful.

Human beings are very good at sniffing out a fake and we just do not trust someone who is closed off.

The second difference was a surprise. The continuing couples argued more than the non-continuing ones. Common sense would dictate that conflict would drive people apart. However, on further reflection, the findings are fascinating. How well long-term couples handle conflict is the single best predictor for relationship success – and it seems the ability to disagree constructively is just as important at five dates as at five years.

How this myth traps you in limbo: Unfortunately, the myth of love at first sight not only makes people turn down good potential partners but can also confuse us and bond us with someone who might seem just right on the first date but turns out to be toxic (more about this in the next chapter). For committed couples, the myth of a passionate start can also become a handicap and make them question the very foundations of their relationship.

'We met at college when my husband was twenty and I was nineteen,' explained Janet, who is now thirty-three. 'What started as a friendship blossomed into a relationship and, apart from a short break in our twenties, we have been together ever since. However, there was no real passion when we met, just excitement about each other's characters and physically it was more experimentation than lust that kept us going. Unfortunately, I'm now looking for a more emotional connection with my husband, which I feel I have the capacity to give, but I'm not receiving anything back. It seems like we can never get away from the immature beginnings of our relationship.' During their counselling, I worked with Janet and her husband to help them understand that friendship and shared interests were just as important a foundation – if not much stronger – than love at first sight.

REASSESS YOUR TEENAGE DREAMS OF LOVE

Cast your mind back to your first serious crush when you became interested in boys or girls.

- **Step into the past.** Remember writing his name in your exercise book or hanging around after school in the hope of seeing her. What did your beloved look like? What smells take you back to that time?
- **Remember your daydreams.** What did you imagine life would be like with your crush? Put as much flesh back on to the daydream as

possible. Where did you imagine living? How many children? What would love be like?

- **Question the dreams.** How realistic were your expectations of love? Are you still holding on to some of those old dreams? Do they in some hidden way inform your life today?
- **Compare reality with the dream.** Instead of worrying about what didn't happen, look at all the ways that reality has been better than your teenage fantasies. If you could travel back in time and meet that schoolboy or schoolgirl, what would you tell them? How has life turned out better than he or she could have hoped?

2. Everybody has a soulmate

Contemporary culture encourages us to concentrate on what we *want* from a relationship. Somehow, if we can just articulate these desires, often in minute detail, we will be one step closer to finding our soulmate and living happily ever after with no major disagreements.

Lydia is in her late thirties with a young child, but has become disillusioned with the men whom she attracted: 'They are all losers in some way. They are attractive but they would drink too much, smoke too much dope, or have money

problems. In effect, they can't look after themselves.' Determined not to make the same mistakes
again, Lydia has drawn up a tick list of requirements. I've added her explanations in italics:

- Aged 38–48. *'Ideally, he should be four years
older than me.'*

- Unconventional. *'The father of my child had
had a very ordinary childhood, so we could never
really understand each other.'*

- Has a chequered past but is now sorted. *'I'm
bored easily and can find "normal" relationships claustrophobic.'*

- Travelled.

- Has read *Stone Junction* by Jim Dodge. *'If
you don't like this book – which is really hippie
and full of magic realism – you don't pass the
test.'*

- Creative.

- The film *Gummo*. *'You don't have to have seen
this film but your reaction is another test. How*

else can I know that you can cope with my darkness?

- Left-field music tastes. *'I like contemporary jazz and funk.'*

- Spiritual but not religious.

- Good tattoos.

- Not possessive.

At first, I thought that Lydia was joking, but she was serious. In fact, she suggested that I include her email address in the book in case someone could tick all the boxes. So I asked whether any of the items were negotiable. 'Perhaps the good tattoos, I can put up with a couple of dodgy ones. But if someone has none at all, I think we'd be too different to click.' Lydia's list reveals a lot about her. So much, in fact, that I started wondering if she was projecting herself on to this soulmate. If this man did exist, he would be almost her twin and the two of them could live in perfect harmony. It sounds great, but what about the reality?

Jeremy, forty-seven, did find his 'soulmate': 'I really did think she was the one. We were both actors, so she understood the pressures. She ticked all the boxes but it turned out to be the most horrible relationship that I've ever been in. She'd been in some abusive relationships and started imagining that I was looking at other women whenever we went out. She'd get incredibly angry and then violent. I even started wondering if she was right that I did have a roving eye and that she'd help me sort it.' As someone who analysed his every thought and action, Jeremy did not need a partner with similar skills but someone practical who would have said: 'That's enough talking, let's get on and do it.' In fact, the relationship with the actress was so traumatic that when it ended, Jeremy was overwhelmed with despair and sought professional help. There will be more from him in the following chapters.

How this myth traps you in limbo: A soulmate who will understand, accept and validate us – just because he or she is simply on the same wavelength – is a very appealing idea. What makes this myth doubly seductive is that if he or she is our soulmate, then automatically we must be his or her soulmate too. Therefore the two of us can come together in some kind of miraculous union – without the hard work of forging a relationship.

By this I mean agonising over whether he or she really likes us, whether it's safe to let down our barriers (showing how needy or frightened we really are), compromising over different needs and learning to communicate properly.

So many people turn down a good prospective man or woman at the first hurdle – because they are not 'soul partners' – rather than waiting that little bit longer, truly getting to know each other and beginning to grow (rather than magically fusing) into great and possibly perfect partners. For people who are already in committed relationships, the myth of soul partners can be equally destructive. Twenty-five years as a marital therapist has shown me that being too similar is almost as bad for a relationship as being too different. These twin couples become like brother and sister or good friends, and all the passion disappears. In effect, we need difference to keep the relationship alive, interesting and growing. Difference is like the grit in an oyster shell – probably annoying for the oyster, but it produces something incredible: a pearl.

So I wonder if a soulmate is actually good for us. Perhaps what we *want* and what we *need* are two different things. Worse still, the myth of a soulmate can make someone in an OK or troubled long-term relationship not only question their love for their partner – because real relationships are complex and sometimes involve hard work – but also start to imagine that a work colleague or friend is actually 'the love of their life'. (If this sounds familiar, please read my book *How Can I Ever Trust You Again?*, which explains how affairs happen in an unreal bubble and the destructive fallout once the bubble bursts.)

EXAMINE YOUR PERSONAL TICK BOXES

This next exercise is especially for someone who is trying to decide whether a new relationship has a future. However, it can still be insightful for someone in a long-term relationship deciding whether to stay or go.

Part one: Compile

- What are all your requirements for a partner? Write each one down and be as specific as possible. For example, don't just write, 'the same age' or 'younger than me'; put in the full acceptable age range.

- Here are some prompts to help you. What about height? Hair colour? What physical characteristics (such as weight, muscular build, size of breasts)? What profession? What salary? What interests? Where does this person live? What about their past? What about their class? What about their family? What about the opinions/requirements of your own family?

- Next look at reasons why you have turned down people who have shown an interest in you in the past. For example, he was wearing a cheap watch or she had a common laugh. Be honest about your prejudices. Whom would you never date? If you are in a long-term relationship, list all the issues that are making you question whether your partner is right for you.

- Factor in past relationships and bad experiences that make you wary of someone with those tastes or traits. Some of these items might seem petty to other people but, if you are honest, are deal-breakers for you. When I did this exercise with Connor, thirty-two, he admitted: 'I always check out the music collection – especially after I dated this girl who had nothing but artists who were famous for one terrible novelty record. I didn't even know that most had even brought out albums until I found them in her home. Not only did it make me seriously question her judgement, but worse, we'd always fight about what we'd listen to on long car journeys.' Another example is Amelia, twenty-eight, who had been out with a man who was a bully. 'He never attacked me, but I had the sense that he might if he didn't get his own way. So I tend to be nervous of big men and especially those with loud voices.'

- Is there anything else to add? Even if it makes you look shallow, put it on your list.

Part two: Compromise
- Having compiled your list, go back and study it. How likely is it that someone will meet all these criteria? When you say: 'I never meet any eligible men' or 'I never meet any nice women', do you really mean that I never meet anyone who ticks *all* my boxes?
- Are there items which, on reflection, seem too restrictive? If so, strike them off your list.
- Next think back to previous relationships: were there any issues which seemed like stumbling blocks but which subsequently you overcame? For example, Amelia did not like people smoking in her flat and refused to date smokers. However, she had got to know Jamie at work and he had sneaked his way into her affections before she knew it. 'We found a way round it; he agreed to go outside for a cigarette and

after six months he cut down to smoking only on Saturday nights if we visited friends who smoked, or went out to a club.' What else could you cross off your list?

- For a moment let's imagine that your partner is a reasonable person. On which items might it be possible to find a compromise? For example, Connor could agree to have his choice of music on alternate car journeys, put on a talk radio station or listen to nothing and just chat. Is there anything else on the list that might be negotiable?

Part three: Challenge

- Look again at your most deeply held convictions. These might seem sacred 'must have' items but are you, in reality, just bowing to received wisdom?
- Does money truly trump every other quality? Is the height of your partner really that important? Is it reasonable to expect your partner to fulfil all your needs?
- What items on your list could you move from prerequisites to preferences?
- At this point, hopefully, your list will be more about your prospective partner's character – intrinsic qualities – than habits, looks and circumstances – extrinsic matters.

3. You can't have too much choice

It goes without saying that the Internet has revolutionised how we communicate and meet people. However, searching for a partner in this way can be soul-destroying. 'You have to go into this with your eyes wide open,' says Erin, a thirty-eight-year-old divorcee. 'There are a lot of fakes, married men and weirdos. I quickly found that a lot of men lie. They knock a few years off their age and add them to their height. It's a bit like drugs in sports – everybody does it – so you join in to level the playing field.'

However, the greatest benefit of meeting online is also the greatest problem: the sheer number of people. With so much choice, you need to come up with quick ways of narrowing your search. Women complain that men want someone at least ten years younger: 'If I went along with that idea, I'd be dating men who were fifty or even fifty-five,' complains Erin, 'but I want to meet men around my own age.' Men's complaint is that women only go for tall men. 'I'm five feet six inches tall,' explains Ben, who is thirty-six, 'but even women five feet nothing to five feet three want a minimum of five feet eight.' Even searching based on common interests, rather than superficial qualities like looks, is problematic and can rule out a good match.

For example, Nathan and Jane have been married for ten years and enjoy teasing each other about their respective tastes. 'He reads these brick-sized books with violent death on every page and he complains that I read boring books, which might win literary prizes, but nothing actually happens in them,' say Jane. 'I enjoy ridiculing his music – normally progressive rock dinosaurs that you thought died a million years ago – but he gets his revenge when he finds me bopping around the kitchen to pop songs on the radio. What is most important is that we laugh and cry over the same things, which I guess is harder to discover in a few emails.' Jane has a point; narrowing your search might cut down the sheer number of messages, but it is only a short step from filtering for practical reasons to believing that your beloved must fulfil a tight number of criteria and simply closing your mind to anyone else.

If you progress from exchanging messages online, to phoning and then meeting in a pub or coffee shop, the virtual world still casts a shadow. Your date will not only be trying to decide if there is a connection between you, but will also be comparing you to all his or her other potential dates. Susan, forty-seven, used lonely hearts columns back in the mid-eighties and following her divorce has embraced Internet dating: 'I always used to feel that I was auditioning rather than dating, that I should be tap dancing past while my date held up a score card for personality, looks and presentation. However, even in popular lonely hearts columns, you would get only a handful of letters – now the possibilities are endless. Sometimes, I wonder if we give each other a chance before we shout "next".'

There is another issue with Internet dating: the sheer amount of time that it can swallow. 'You have to be careful or you are online all evening,' explains Susan. 'I'll promise myself that I'll just check my messages and before I know it, I've been at the computer for a couple of hours. It's sort of addictive – so I ration myself.' However, when she'd had a tough time at work, she would 'reward' herself with a couple of hours of flirting. 'It really gives you a lift that some guy whom you really fancy has "tagged" your profile, and a text from a potential date after a tough meeting, where nobody is prepared to listen, can help power you through the afternoon. But I've decided to come offline for a while. I realised that I might be "meeting" lots of guys but I wasn't getting to know any of them. For the first couple of days, I felt rather jittery – perhaps Mr Right had sent me a message – but I held my nerve and I've been surprised at how calm I feel. I can finally concentrate on my work and friends again.' It is important to realise that Internet dating can be a mood-altering quick fix – just like alcohol, caffeine, chocolate and other substances that are fine in moderation but cause problems in excess.

How this myth traps you in limbo: On paper it should be true that the more people you date, the greater the likelihood of clicking with someone. However, I am seeing an increasing number of people who have over-dated. 'I decided to really go for it and go on as many dates as possible,' says Brooke, who is thirty-eight. 'They might not all be successful or even enjoyable but I'd at least have a better idea of what I want.' At her peak, she managed to fit in three dates a week and, on occasion, met a different man at lunchtime and in the evening at the same wine bar. 'I'm not certain if the look on the waiter's face was surprise, admiration or sympathy.' Unfortunately, Brooke ended up confused and burnt out. Her experience was replicated by researchers at the Columbia Business

School, who set up two stalls at a supermarket offering tastings of exotic jams. The first stall had just six varieties, while the second had twenty-four. The larger choice attracted more customers, but just 3 per cent used a money-off voucher to purchase the jam. With the smaller range, 30 per cent of the tasters were converted into buyers. So why was the group with more choice not satisfied? Greater choice actually diminishes our enjoyment because we fear that amongst the discarded options is something that we might have liked more.

REASSESS YOUR INTERNET DATING HABITS

Take a look at the following questions and total up the number that you agree with:

1. Do you feel increased tension and excitement when there is the possibility of a new online hook-up?
2. Do you find yourself looking forward to going online?
3. Do you plan your life around going online?
4. When you're out socialising with friends, do you find yourself thinking about what you might be missing online?

5. Do you ever have text conversations with a potential hook-up even though you are out socialising with friends?

6. Is your online flirting and hunting a reward for the stress that you endure?

7. Do you find that after making a conquest, you can begin to lose interest and start searching for someone else?

8. Does the flattery of strangers – even though you suspect it might not be sincere – still make you feel better about yourself?

9. Can life online help you forget about other problems?

10. Do you sometimes only truly feel yourself when you are online?

11. Do you disguise or tell white lies about the amount of time you spend online?

12. Have you ever chatted up someone online that you don't really fancy or someone that other people might find disgusting?

13. Do you find yourself repeatedly on your favourite dating site longer than you expected?

14. If you wake up in the middle of the night, do you go and check your messages?

15. Are you afraid that life will become unbearably dull and boring when you get older and that fewer people will find you attractive?

16. Has a friend, family member or work colleague expressed serious concern about the amount of time that you spend online or your dating habits?

17. Would you instinctively understand someone who said 'yes' to most of these questions?

Scoring your answers: This questionnaire is designed to get you thinking rather than provide a point where you pass – and have no problems – or fail and should take action. However, you should be concerned if you answered 'yes' to more than four or five questions.

Understanding your score: I've adapted this questionnaire from those used to assess people with addictive personalities who have developed a cross-addiction; it looks at patterns of behaviour rather than just the amounts or frequency of use of mood-altering substances or pastimes. In particular: **Preoccupation** (tested in questions 1–5), **Use for effect** and **Use as medicine** (tested in questions 6–10), **Protection of supply** (tested in questions 11 and 12), **Using more than planned** (tested in questions 13 and 14) and **Higher capacity than others** (tested in questions 15–17).

What action to take: First of all, I think there should be a disclaimer. There is a big difference between abusing alcohol, drugs or sex (which have serious health impacts on the sufferer and cause distress to their families) and spending too long online or compulsive dating. However, I believe that this behaviour can be counter-productive to your search for a committed partner. So what should you do? It is probably time to take a break and consider different ways of meeting people. Anyone who has had a serious addiction problem, and scored highly on this test, should consider getting advice from their doctor or returning to their twelve-step programme.

4. Great sex equals a great relationship

The sixties sexual revolution gave women permission to enjoy sex just as much as men – something that has improved relationships no end – but it has had the side effect that some women reversed an old trick. Today I am more likely to counsel women who offer sex as a way of starting a relationship than those who withhold it. Our new understanding of how the brain works – from PET scans, MRIs, endocrinological studies and galvanic skin-response tests – offers some explanation for this strategy. Male oxytocin levels – the bonding chemical – are lower than women's; except for one moment: ejaculation.

However, there is a big difference between sleeping with someone and laying the foundations for a lasting relationship. Both offering and with-holding sex starts a relationship off with game playing and is detrimental in the long term. You can trick someone into being interested, but only temporarily; eventually he or she will cotton on and wake up disillusioned. The secret of knowing when to agree to sex and when to pass, lies in a proper understanding of how two people bond, and working with the process:

1. When two strangers meet, their subconscious will start checking whether there are comple-mentary needs or the skills to make each other complete. Give this process plenty of time and do not rush into bed too soon.
2. Sex is so powerful that it can short-circuit this delicate matching and bond two people who are not necessarily compatible or who have different agendas.
3. Trust your instincts – rather than the opinions of your friends – they are there for a purpose.
4. Remember that sex means different things to

different people. For one partner, great passion in the bedroom might be a sign of falling in love for ever and ever. For the other partner, wonderful sex could be an end in itself.

5. If you suspect that you and your boyfriend or girlfriend have fundamentally different attitudes – especially if he or she arrives shortly before making love and leaves soon afterwards or cannot find the time for proper courting – test the waters by withholding once or twice. This will soon provide clarification and avoid long-term misery.

What about sex in settled relationships? Here the myth works in the opposite direction and becomes 'If we're not having good sex, then we can't have a good relationship'. However, there can be a multitude of reasons why sex is disappointing: depression, redundancy, birth of a baby and general ignorance. Donna and Allan were on the verge of splitting up when they started counselling because their sex life had dwindled to almost nothing. 'He gets sulky and moody if I'm not up for it – and, with a small baby, that seldom happens – so I'll just think, "Get on and get it over with",' explained Donna. 'To be honest, if we never had sex again it wouldn't bother me.' Allan was in despair: 'If my wife doesn't fancy me, what's the point of carrying on?'

Women experience a seismic shift in their levels of desire after having a baby but unfortunately men expect nothing to change. In fact, it will take a woman two years after giving birth for her hormone levels to return to normal and to feel spontaneously horny again. In the meantime, men like Allan feel unloved – sex was Allan's main way of expressing affection. Donna had been avoiding all physical contact, in case it gave Allan wrong signals, so I helped them learn the joy of a cuddle for its own sake. Ten to fifteen minutes on the sofa – with lots of stroking each other – not only helped Donna unwind after a hard day with the baby but also showed Allan that he was still valued. There is more on boosting intimacy in another book in this series: *Build a Life-long Love Affair*.

How this myth traps you in limbo: It is human nature to compare and test our relationship against our friends' or neighbours'. While the degree to which our partner loves us is hard to measure, we can count up how often we have sex. However, frequency of intercourse is a very crude way of measuring the health of our relationship. I have met too many toxic couples who have been blinded by passion in the bedroom, and many others with good relationships but who are suffering from sexual boredom, to see quality of lovemaking as a reliable sign of the viability of a relationship.

TOP THREE WAYS TO TALK ABOUT SEX

It is much easier to be honest if you follow these golden rules:

- **Keep it positive.** Build on what is good rather than complain about what is wrong. For example: 'I like it when you're gentle' (rather than 'You're too rough').
- **Talk in the living room.** Discussing problems in the bedroom, especially after sex, makes the topic more loaded and more personal. By contrast, talking in the living room or kitchen turns sex into a normal everyday subject.
- **Be specific.** Instead of talking in generalities (for example: 'I'm worried about the amount of intimacy') focus on concrete things that you can change (for example: 'I wish we had long, lingering kisses').

5. I shouldn't have to tell you

This is one of the most destructive myths about relationships and although it can affect new or emerging couples, it is particularly pernicious for long-term couples. At the beginning of a relationship, we spend a lot of time telling our beloved all our hopes and fears. In an ideal world, we would be this connected all the time. However, we also have livings to earn, houses to maintain and children to bring up. It's not that our partner stops caring but rather becomes preoccupied with some crisis: an overdue report, a child caught using drugs or the pile of laundry waiting to be ironed.

If you and your partner have been together for many years, it is easy to forget just how much both of you will have changed. What we needed and wanted at twenty is not the same as at thirty, forty or fifty. Unfortunately, many couples are still working on old assumptions from when they first met and just expect their partner to 'know' what has changed.

Lizzie and George were in their late forties and had been together for ten years. She had two children from a previous relationship and they also had a seven-year-old daughter together. Lizzie's first husband had been abusive and her childhood had been difficult too. Although George was open about his problem – a lack of closeness – Lizzie was withdrawn in the counselling room and it took several weeks for her to open up. 'We talked a lot when we first met and I thought George was someone that I could trust,' she explained, 'but when there's a problem he just walks away and I feel rejected and alone. At least if I was single I'd know where I was. I could get on with things.' George looked shocked; he'd had no idea she'd been thinking about splitting up: 'You get so upset if we row, it always seemed better to avoid rows but I never knew that you felt this way. You can't trust me?' She nodded. 'Why didn't you tell me?' he asked. 'I thought that if you really loved me you would know,' Lizzie added. It sounded to me like a test that she'd given him, and I said so. 'I haven't thought of it like that, but yes, you're right, and George kept failing, which sort of confirmed that I was right not to open up,' she explained. George exploded: 'I'm not a mind-reader.'

How this myth traps you in limbo: Instead of putting the focus on something that you can change – such as poor communication – this myth makes you wait for your partner to act. No wonder you feel disempowered and in limbo. However, there is good news. Once you start talking, your relationship will come on in leaps and bounds.

DEAL WITH THE PINCHES

Whenever our partner does something annoying – like leaving an empty coffee cup in the living room – but we say nothing, it is being 'pinched': a minor irritation that we shrug off. However, if you are pinched enough times it becomes impossible to contain your annoyance any longer: you have cashed in your 'pinch' for a 'crunch'.

- For the next twenty-four hours, monitor how many times you are pinched. Don't do anything, just be aware of your reaction and how you feel inside.
- Next, experiment with dealing with the pinches. Ask your partner, for example, to put the used cup in the dishwasher. Make certain that you ask straight away and keep the request to this one case.
- Finally, reassess the way that you deal with pinches. Does dealing with the small issues stop them from escalating into big ones? How could your communication with your partner be improved?

Summing Up

When a relationship gets trapped in limbo, there is often an unchallenged myth that has come between a couple and opened up a huge chasm. When one partner believes, for example, in 'soul partners' and the other falls short of this ideal, there is little incentive to talk about the problem (because what can the second partner do about it?) or to work on the relationship (because where would you start?). In many cases, once the myth is exploded and couples start really talking about their issues, it soon becomes clear whether a relationship has a future or not.

IN A NUTSHELL:

- Think about all the beliefs you have about yourself, relationships and life in general.
- Where do they come from? How valid are they? Do they need updating?
- How could you improve communication between you and your partner?

STEP 2

LOOK AT
YOUR PARTNER

It takes two people to make a couple and however much you change or work on your relationship, there is a limit to what you can achieve on your own. In this chapter, I am going to ask you to step back and take a long dispassionate look at the man or woman in your life. My second question is:

What kind of person is your partner?

When I'm working through this programme with clients, I find people stuck in limbo come up with very black-and-white answers: 'He is wonderful' or 'She drives me up the wall'. At first glance, this makes decision-making very straightforward. If you love him then stay. If she is manipulative then go. However, what always happens is that my clients swing back the other way – so it becomes . . .

'He is wonderful but he's got a terrible temper and sometimes I'm frightened of him' or 'She drives me up the wall, I never know what to expect but when we make up after a row, the sex is incredible.'

There is a less dramatic version of this see-saw for long-established couples: 'He's a good man and very caring but there is no passion between us' or 'She's a great mother but we want different things out of life.'

So how do you stop swinging backwards and forwards between feeling positive and then negative? The answer is to look beneath the surface, understand what's really going on and find some greyness amongst the black and white.

How to Spot if Your New Lover is 'Too Good to Be True'

It is around the three-month point that cracks can begin to appear in what, up to this point, might have seemed a perfect relationship. The temptation is to ignore the warning signs and enjoy the passion and the romance – but this would be a big mistake because some potential partners are dangerous.

Although most of my advice is applicable to everyone, this next point is specifically for women. Stockholm Syndrome was named after a bank siege in the capital city of Sweden in the 1970s, where kidnappers and hostages bonded to such an extent that afterwards one woman became engaged to a gunman, while another launched a legal fund to pay for the robbers' defence. This is an extreme example of what is becoming an increasingly common phenomenon: smart women who become willingly trapped in relationships with bad, dangerous or abusive men. So how does it happen and why should you be on your guard?

On the surface, Stockholm Syndrome man is wonderful. He makes dramatic romantic gestures (like buying wildly expensive presents), he is impulsive ('Let's drive down to London, as I know this wonderful little restaurant') and he enjoys breaking the rules ('Who cares what people think?'). While many men fight shy of commitment, Stockholm Syndrome man is the complete opposite, as Michelle, twenty-eight, discovered when she first met Alex, in his late thirties: 'On our second date, he announced that he'd never met anybody like me, I was the love of his life and he was teasing me about what to call our second child,' she remembers. Naturally, she was flattered and began to entertain similar feelings. 'He followed it up with flowers, a stuffed hippo and a weekend in the Cotswolds.' Stockholm Syndrome men do not so much kidnap women but ambush their emotions. 'I was on an incredible high,' explained Michelle, 'it seemed almost too good to be true.' Indeed it was. While it is normal to fall in love quickly, most people hold back until they are certain. By contrast, Stockholm Syndrome men are not afraid of a quick commitment. They make unrealistic promises, have a whole future planned out after a handful of dates, and some even move in during the first month. Alex's grand gestures made Michelle feel like she was in a romantic movie, so she ignored behaviour that would normally have made her suspicious. 'On our way to the Cotswolds, he kept blowing his horn and accusing the driver in the car ahead of being a creep. At the hotel, the room wasn't quite ready and he made a terrible fuss. He was rude to the girl on reception but I didn't like to say anything because he was being so generous.'

Although Michelle recognised that Alex had a temper, and hated not getting his own way, she never thought his fury would be directed at her.

After all, he had told her she was his princess and nothing was too much trouble. What Michelle did not realise was that Alex had started the classic Stockholm Syndrome pattern: fear and reward.

Not every Stockholm Syndrome man becomes violent towards their partner. Some just throw things or get into fights with other men. In this case, Alex spent a night in a prison cell after another man in a nightclub looked at Michelle in what he considered to be a 'funny way'.

The goal is to put the woman on her guard and, therefore, she is easily controlled. Ultimately, all Stockholm Syndrome men become emotionally abusive. 'Because Mike really loved me and wanted the best for me,' explains Josie, thirty-two, 'he would be honest about what he thought.' However, this included insults about her flabby arms, the small roll of flesh round her stomach and her taste in clothes.

So why didn't Josie just leave him? 'If he went too far, he'd be really sweet: breakfast in bed, turning up at the office to take me out for an expensive lunch, jewellery . . . I felt that was the real him and if I tried harder, it could be like that all the time.' Mike was exhibiting the second classic Stockholm Syndrome behaviour: alternating fix and withdrawal.

The bad behaviour in public begins to isolate the woman and, like the hostages in the bank, they are cut off from the outside world. Certainly Josie decided it was too much trouble taking Mike on office outings and, as she explains, 'He always claimed we were happier, just the two of us.' Slowly Josie gave up all her outside interests – such as horse riding – as Mike would insist on coming too and hanging around with a long face and taking all the pleasure from her hobby. He had an issue with her family, too. After a call from her mother, Mike would launch into twenty questions, picking away at the conversation for criticism – real or imagined. So Josie would only phone her family when he was not around: 'He thought Mum took advantage and didn't understand the "special nature of our love".' Mike had put in place another key ingredient for a Stockholm Syndrome relationship: the enemy.

The common foe intensifies the bond between captor and victim. Worse still, with nobody outside to question what is 'normal', women trapped in Stockholm Syndrome relationships put the problems down to their own behaviour. Indeed, Michelle felt Alex behaved badly because: 'I didn't do enough to make him feel safe, didn't make enough sacrifices.' She even felt she was lucky to have someone who put up with her – as, by this time, she felt inadequate and worthless.

So what drives these men? Although a few consciously set out to capture women, most genuinely think they are great guys. Through their eyes, they are very romantic and passionate (but it can get out of hand and become fisticuffs) and their strong sense of entitlement is just an extreme version of our society's self-centredness (I'm in a hurry, so it doesn't matter if my poor parking holds up everybody else). The problem is that these men have an almost pathological inability to understand anybody else's viewpoint or the impact of their behaviour. This makes them permanently right and everybody else permanently in the wrong.

How do you spot a Stockholm Syndrome man?

- Give him the waitress test. Does he whine, complain, torment and generally treat her like dirt?
- What about his ex? Does he tell stories about a mad, angry, stupid or ungrateful woman?
- Does he give reassurances that you didn't ask

for? For example, he never gets drunk or would never actually hit a woman.

- Is he proud of bad behaviour? Like claiming to be a 'butt kicker' at work or doing 'crazy' things such as hanging around outside a girl's apartment all night?
- What about his friends? Stockholm Syndrome men have only acquaintances or a handful of friends who are just like them.

I have yet to come across a woman employing the techniques of Stockholm Syndrome. However, there are other personality traits that are superficially attractive, but deadly for relationships, which are exhibited by both men and women, and which I'll look at next.

The Lure of the Narcissist

Narcissistic Personality Disorder is when someone has a grandiose sense of self-importance and flies into fits of rage at every knock to their self-esteem. Worse still, their extreme form of self-love prevents them from having meaningful relationships with anybody else. The American Psychiatric Association believes that about 0.7 to 1 per cent of the population are sufferers and that the majority of them are men. Five or more of the following would suggest that your new man or, possibly, woman is a sufferer:

1. Has a grandiose sense of self-importance.
2. Preoccupied with fantasies of unlimited success, power, brilliance, beauty or idealised love.
3. Believes that they are special and should only associate with special, high-level people.
4. Needs excessive admiration.
5. Has a sense of entitlement.
6. Exploits others.
7. Lacks empathy.
8. Envious of others or thinks they are envious of him.
9. Haughty, arrogant behaviour.

Narcissists spend a lot of time and money on their appearance. On the surface, they are very confident, and confidence is very attractive. Narcissists' relationships – like everything else about them – must be the best: more intense, passionate and rewarding than everyone else's. For this reason, they throw all their considerable energy into conquering their prospective partner and convincing them that this is the love of the century. It is little wonder that narcissists find it easy to attract prospective partners. Except they are incapable of giving real love and use relationships to inflate their egos. Ultimately, these are hollow men and women and best avoided.

STOP SIGNS: FIVE EARLY WARNING SIGNALS THAT SHOULD BRING YOU UP SHORT

1. **At the beginning, did he or she say: 'I'm not really interested in a relationship right now'?**
   It's amazing how often people tell the truth at the very start. Sometimes they feel we have a right to know and if we ignore the warning, that's our 'lookout', but mainly because at this point the stakes are low and there is no reason to deceive.
   STOP: You're not really listening or only choosing to hear what you want to hear.

2. **Do you make all the running?** What would happen if you didn't call, make plans or find excuses for dropping round? If you stopped, would you hardly ever see him or her?
   STOP: Your relationship is out of balance.

3. **Do you find yourself making excuses for him or her?** Do you feel the need to say that he's 'not always like that' or 'she's had a tough upbringing'? Do you downplay bad behaviour as 'passionate'? STOP: Your friends are worried about you.

4. **Does something not quite add up?** Does he disappear for a few days for no real reason? Have you repeatedly caught her lying about little things? Could your partner be still emotionally entangled with an ex? STOP: No trust, no relationship.

5. **Does he or she always have to win?** When you argue, does your partner stop at nothing – including cruel remarks – to get their own way? Does it seem that he doesn't take your opinions seriously? Does she get upset out of all proportion if you give the 'wrong' answer? STOP: Relationships need give and take.

Déjà-vu

Sometimes a new lover can start to behave just like your old lovers. It is not only depressing to repeat the same arguments, but it can also make you seriously question the viability of your new relationship. So have you fallen for another identikit partner or is déjà-vu magnifying your problems?

Philippa, twenty-eight, had dated a man who had been unfaithful: 'He became very friendly with a girl at the office where we both worked and eventually he admitted he had feelings for her. After a lot of soul searching, I decided to fight for him. Although the other girl backed off, the magic had gone and we drifted apart. I was very hurt and felt a complete fool. No man was worth that sort of knock to my pride.'

Six months later, she started dating Darren. 'It was going really well and we spent most weekends together. However, one Friday morning, he phoned and said he didn't think he would be able to make it back that evening. His job, in TV production down south, was overrunning. Although I was upset, at least he'd had enough respect to warn me – because I hate last-minute cancellations. We agreed to speak later and see what time he finished. I didn't hear anything. I tried phoning but his phone was switched off. Probably, he was stuck in the edit suite. After work, I dropped into the pub not far from home – where we'd first met. My older brother, who runs the place, told me that Darren had been in. I thought: Great, he's back home, we can go out after all. So I called his mobile, but it was still switched off. I kept trying all night and still nothing. I felt so betrayed. What else could it be but another woman?' As it turned out, Darren had been offered a ticket to a football match and, knowing what Philippa's reaction would be, he pretended to be still down south. Déjà-vu had made Philippa assume the worst, rather than waiting to get the facts. They talked over their problems, and Darren agreed not to hide behind white lies and Philippa to be more flexible about changing plans – if there was a good reason.

If you find yourself overreacting to something your partner says or does, stop and think: does it have an extra punch because of something that happened in the past? With intractable problems, I normally reckon that 20 per cent is about today and 80 per cent about your childhood. So look back and unhook the bits that belong to the past. For example, Justine decided to stop trying to police how much her boyfriend drank: 'I might have felt responsible for my dad's behaviour when I was a girl. But now I've grown up, I realise that I can't be responsible for my boyfriend – however much I love him. He has to take charge of his own drinking. It certainly makes life less stressful for me.' Although the problem had not changed, Justine's way of approaching it had changed – with a knock-on effect on the atmosphere in the house. 'I stopped panicking every time he opened the fridge, and with it being less of an issue, he drank less. I also began to see that although my boyfriend sometimes drank too much, unlike my dad, he did not have a serious problem.'

If our partner's behaviour is making us unhappy, our first reaction is always to try and get them to change. But in the rush, we forget about our own contribution, our own history and how we might be projecting past problems on to our new relationship. By behaving differently, the chances are that our partner will react differently too.

So if you suspect déjà-vu, step back and ask: in what other ways could I approach this problem? If you can't think of anything different, ask your friends or try the opposite of your normal tactics – anything that breaks the old cycle, makes you see your partner as an individual and stops past relationships overshadowing what is happening today.

The other key to breaking old patterns is hanging on a little longer. Often when we are arguing with our partner, we think the relationship is in trouble but, actually, fights are a sign of hope. This is particularly the case with déjà-vu. If most of our big problems have their roots in the past, today's fights are a way of solving, by proxy, those long-standing issues. Even if you suspect an identikit partner, in 90 per cent of cases it is better to hang on and give yourself time to try and solve the problems.

CHANGE THE PATTERNS AND CHANGE THE RELATIONSHIP

If you find yourself falling for the same kind of man or woman over and over again, it is helpful to understand why these people hold such a strong fascination for you:

1. Go through your photograph album and choose a picture which seems to encapsulate the personality of every significant man or woman in your life – from your father or mother to the present day. Stretch them out side by side: what are the similarities and what are the patterns?

2. Ask yourself the following questions: How did I behave? What did I expect? Did I try too hard

to please? Who was in charge? How did I try and solve arguments?

3. Identify other ways to be around men/women. If you have sons, this is a great way to learn about men. If you have daughters, this is a great way to learn about women. Do you have any platonic friends of the opposite sex? What about male or female work colleagues? Look for alternative ways of reacting and rehearse in these safe relationships.

4. Make subtle changes in your relationship with your parents. For example, rather than resolving to make big changes like 'stand on my own two feet', start with something more specific, for example: organise your car finance package your-self. Not only are small changes easier to maintain but also the cumulative effect is impressive.

5. If your father or mother is dead, or has disap-peared, write an imaginary letter telling him or her all your feelings.

No Chemistry

This problem can affect both couples who are just starting out and those who have been together for years. 'I desperately want to love this guy as we are great friends and get on, but I've never felt that passionate about him,' explained Rita, twenty-eight. 'I didn't want to spend every moment with him and never felt like I was floating on air – like when you normally fall in love. I do miss him and I always wished I could be happy and in love with him.' In a new or emerging relationship, a lack of chemistry probably says more about you than your potential partner. Indeed, Rita had just finished another relationship and she kept stopping herself from falling in love. Other people are frightened of being hurt and therefore only date people for whom they have no strong feelings.

'In my experience, if the fancying component is downplayed, the resisting component is turned up,' explained Jeremy, the actor who'd had a violent 'soul partner'. His next relationship was with Freya. 'I found her attractive but I was not besotted. She was lovely, caring and supportive but I kept resisting her. She didn't fit my normal taste of slim, dark-eyed and dark-haired women.' After eight months, Jeremy ended the relationship because 'she was too nice and did not challenge me'.

Sometimes a couple can be together for years but one partner begins to feel that they have nothing in common or they have turned from lovers into brother and sister. Howard and Natalie, who were thirty-six and thirty-four, had been together since their teens and had two sons aged nine and six. They sought my help because Howard had lost all his passion for Natalie: 'I just don't want to come home. If I can find an excuse to go somewhere else or do something else, I will. We just have nothing in common any more.' Natalie started listing shared friends, opinions on how to raise their boys and sharing a bath together most days: 'And it's not like we argue or don't get on,' she said. Howard sighed: 'There's no chemistry, and when you've lost the love, you can't get it back.'

By not arguing, the couple had been suppressing their feelings. It started with anger and upset and then spread to joy and love. The answer, surprisingly, is a good row. It brings all the issues up to the surface and couples begin to say what they feel rather than what they think their partner wants to hear. There is more advice on this in my book *I Love You But I'm Not In Love With You* (published by Bloomsbury).

Another common situation for long-term couples is where a build-up of resentment has created a barrier and thereby destroyed any chemistry. 'I need to be appreciated more and not taken for granted,' said Sally, who is fifty and wrote to my website. 'My husband has done nothing at all in all the years to make me feel valued: never books dinner or a babysitter; the few times that we've been away together I have had to take the initiative. Even on our twentieth wedding anniversary, he discussed it with me and we jointly arranged our weekend away. We don't talk in any way that is meaningful to me or emotionally satisfying. We are like flatmates discussing work and kids. Our sex life is non-existent – but that's because over the years I have not been interested when all I get by way of foreplay is a bit of heavy breathing at 11.30 p.m. after the football has finished. I am so resentful of his apparent lack of enthusiasm to engage in trying to change things.' We expect a lot from our relationships these days and Sally is not just asking to be appreciated but for her husband to make her feel valued.

However much someone loves us, they cannot be responsible for making us feel good about ourselves or propping up our self-esteem – that ultimately is our own responsibility. Sometimes letting go of this expectation will lower the temperature and allow you and your partner to communicate better and start repairing your relationship.

FIVE SIGNS TO CARRY ON: YOUR RELATIONSHIP IS WORTH TRYING TO SAVE IF . . .

1. **You have children together.** Although we hope children quickly recover from divorce, long-term tracking shows that most are still wrestling with the fallout five, ten and even twenty-five years later.

   CARRY ON: Unless there is violence or there are addiction problems, most children want their parents to stay together.

2. **You respect and value your partner's opinions.** Putting aside recent bad behaviour – like an affair – if you have compatible values, there is a good foundation for the future.

   CARRY ON: Compatibility is one of the key ingredients for a long-term relationship.

3. **You have a basic friendship.** Sometimes, couples use this reason to split – fearing that

they might lose their friendship if things turn nasty – but my experience is that their friendship is actually protecting the relationship from misunderstandings and spiteful behaviour.

CARRY ON: Friendship is never spoilt by genuinely trying to solve problems, only by ignoring them.

4. **Your partner is committed to your relationship.** Even if it seems that your partner only wants to stay together out of habit or familiarity, this can be enough of a spur to change if he or she genuinely thinks the relationship is in danger.

CARRY ON: Does your partner know how truly unhappy you are or have you been holding back for fear of hurting him or her?

5. **You've yet to seek professional help.** People think they've tried everything but normally have just used a more extreme version of their old failed way of resolving disputes – like shouting louder or sulking longer.

CARRY ON: A professional counsellor will bring a fresh perspective and new ways of communicating.

Summing Up

When we meet someone new, we can be too busy looking for reasons why we should like them rather than looking for reasons why we shouldn't. So sometimes we close our eyes, rationalise away or downplay important pieces of evidence. Conversely, when we are angry or resentful towards a long-term partner, we can act like a small child expecting him or her to sort out our problems – more like a parent than a lover. This trap makes us feel helpless or, if we do take action, again it can be like a small child – throwing a tantrum – rather than using our adult skills of discussing, looking for solutions and finding compromises.

Whether you are downplaying or exaggerating failings, the result is an overly black or white picture of your partner. A better way to make a decision is to explore both extremes, and all the graduations in between. In this way, you are making a judgement on the whole person, not a partial view.

IN A NUTSHELL:

- Are you in love with your partner or just his or her potential?
- How available is your new man or woman for a relationship?
- Have you been expecting your partner to make you feel good about yourself rather than taking responsibility for your own happiness?

STEP 3

LOOK AT YOURSELF

When something goes wrong, it might be human nature to look around for someone else to blame, but while criticising our partner or new lover, we don't have to face up to our own contribution. Although we might protect our self-esteem, this strategy stops us learning from our experiences. So this next step is all about looking at your part in the problem. My third question is:

What's holding you back from making a decision?

Sometimes the answer to this question can be lack of information but, more often, it is something deeper: we would rather be in limbo than confront something painful about our current circumstances or something disturbing from our past.

Single Life Today

There are times in everybody's life when being single makes sense. During an intensive time of study or a leap up the career ladder, moving to a new city and putting down roots and, most commonly, after a relationship break-up. For example, Sophie, fifty-two, has been single for four years since the messy break-up of her marriage. 'There's nobody in my life at the moment but I'm not looking. I put a lot of energy into my work and one of my sons has just bought his first flat. So I've been helping him furnish it and move in. I'm always busy. To tell you the truth, I'm rather enjoying pleasing just myself. I can decide what to watch on the television, what pictures go on my wall and if I want to just read, there is nobody to tell me I'm being selfish. I still do many of the things that I did with my ex-husband – like going to galleries, the theatre and the opera – but I either go with friends or by myself. I might be alone quite a lot but I'm not lonely.'

Sophie has found a good resting place for now between the past and the future. So ask yourself: Are my doubts about my new partner simply that I am not ready for a new relationship yet? This is particularly likely if you have just come out of a long-term relationship and need time to lick your wounds and recover. (There is more advice on this in another book in this series: *Heal and Move On*.)

For most people, the doubts about their new partner are more complex. Being single might be easier today than in the past – and that is something we need to celebrate – but I am always struck by how hard it still remains. Lorna is thirty-eight and has recently married, but she shudders when she looks back. 'I don't think people in rela tionships understand how exhausting it is to be single – especially for women. You have to ruthlessly plan your social life or you can be left looking at a long empty weekend of nothing. The weekdays are not too difficult. I'd be tired after work or I'd take an aerobics class; alternatively, it would be a girl friend's birthday and a group of us would go out for a meal. However, Friday night to Sunday night belonged to my friends' boyfriends, partners and husbands – so it could be an empty, dull void.'

On the surface, single men have it easier than single women. Even today, it is easier for a man to walk into a pub on his own, and football matches and other sporting occasions provide plenty of casual contacts. However, beer is at the centre of each of these activities and while filling the empty hours many men develop a drinking habit that repels potential partners.

Coping Strategies that Can Backfire

Although much of the stigma of being single has disappeared, it still remains tough. Worse still, many of the tricks that single people use to take the edge off what Lorna calls the 'void' make things worse. In effect, these coping strategies fill the hours – and therefore work in the short and medium term – but often become a trap:

1. Friends as surrogate partners

Balancing the needs of your partner and those of your friends is always difficult, especially if your relationship is still at the courting/dating stage. Carol and Alice, both in their mid-thirties, had been flatmates for three years. 'Alice was not just someone to go out with, but, more important, someone to stay in with on a Saturday night,' explained Carol. 'But when I met my future husband, who liked clubbing, I felt that I was betraying her by leaving her behind. When she came too, she felt like a gooseberry and, anyway, she doesn't like clubs.' Often it seemed that Alice was subtly trying to undermine Carol's relationship but Carol stuck to her guns and put her boyfriend first. This is important during the early days of a relationship – which I call blending – where each potential partner has to let their barriers down. Normally, there is a lot of lust, passion and love – which helps – but unless a couple spend enough time alone together it is impossible to build up the trust necessary to let someone truly into your life.

Unfortunately, I counsel many single people who use their commitment to a circle of friends to keep potential lovers at arm's length. Although it is annoying for friends when you have less time, it can ultimately be in everybody's best interest. Shortly after Carol met her future husband, Alice started going out more and married eighteen months after her friend.

As well as friends as surrogate partners, I have met single men and women who have used their children in the surrogate role – taking them out for an evening in a fancy restaurant – and their aged parents. Whoever takes the role, the effect is the same. This relationship takes such precedence that budding love affairs are starved of oxygen and never truly get started.

2. Comfort dating

To ward off feelings of loneliness, some people ensure that they always have a love interest – even if it is nothing very serious. Women who comfort date often choose an older man who will take them places and entertain lavishly. Men choose women who perhaps have children and are pleased to lay an extra place for Sunday lunch. Comfort dates are just something to be going on with; a bit of light-hearted fun until something better comes along.

In some ways, there is nothing wrong with this strategy – especially if the other person knows not to take things too seriously. However, relationships seldom stand still, simple affection grows into something stronger and someone gets hurt. Alexandra, thirty-seven, had been seeing Leo, fifty-two, for four months. They had been to the theatre, spent a bank holiday Monday by the sea and shared a bed together. 'One Sunday morning we had a long cuddle. It felt really nice to be held,' explains Alexandra, 'but he seemed tearful and after a bit of coaxing confessed: "I know this is not for ever but please let me stay around until you find someone else." It was like he was holding up a sign saying "kick me" and I felt so ashamed of myself. I'd been using him and it made me feel all dirty inside.' This comfort-dating relationship had become damaging for both partners' self-esteem.

The gay world has a twist on the casual-but-repeat rendezvous, except that their version skips the date part and heads straight to the bedroom. It's called f**k buddies. Over the past five years or so, this phenomenon has spread to the hetero-sexual world too. In effect, two consenting adults enjoy straightforward recreational sex; there are 'no strings' but a friendship to add an extra layer of intimacy. It sounds fine but often works better in theory than in practice. 'Toby was involved with someone else but we had our Wednesday nights – when he was supposed to be at his Spanish class,' explains Phoebe, twenty-eight. 'Our relationship was all about the sex – it was like a workout between the sheets. It got my pulse racing and put a smile on my face that lasted until the weekend.' However, sex has a way of binding two people together and Phoebe found she was enjoying chatting and sharing a bottle of wine as much as the lovemaking. 'I found myself resenting the fact that he didn't call, that we never went anywhere – he was frightened of being spotted with me. In short, I started acting like his mistress.' Phoebe had fallen in love and became embroiled in an affair that lasted eighteen months.

Although comfort dating and f**k buddies might seem a harmless way to fill the void, it can leave everyone with even more emotional baggage.

3. Living behind a shield

Although it makes sense to take time out while recovering from a painful break-up, some people are so traumatised that they choose to opt out permanently. Jessica is in her fifties. I've known her for about ten years, and over that time she has never mentioned a partner or even an interest in one. In fact, she has often told me that women over fifty are virtually invisible and, as a writer, she enjoys the chance to watch without being observed. Indeed, I think of her as having a permanent sheet of Plexiglas between herself and men. She talks to them and they talk to her but there is a barrier that stops the unspoken communion that builds attraction and desire. So has she truly retired?

'I've been writing in a bar close to where I live; the food is cheap and good quality and there's a quiet corner in the organ loft – it used to be a church. Normally, there is nobody up there, but a few weeks ago I saw this guy reading a book – at a table at the opposite end,' Jessica explained. 'Being curious, I peeked a look at the book – something about science – when he went down to get another drink. The next two times that I went in, there he was at the same table with the same book. It felt too much of a coincidence. The third time, he was not there. I was deep in a screenplay and when I looked up from my laptop, he was there at the table next to me. I was so startled that I looked down immediately. When I left, I thought about saying something – "Still reading the same book" – but he buried his face in his paperback.' As Jessica told the story, I could sense, for the first time, her longing to connect. There had probably been countless other men who were interested but whom Jessica did not notice or whom she was too shy to encourage.

As it turns out, Jessica had a bad experience – a relationship with a man who became violent – and her top priority has been safety. She dare not let her Plexiglas defence down in case she gets hurt again. This strategy has been a great success; she has remained safe but alone. In fact, it has become so much a part of her that she was not aware of it. She was probably even a little shocked that I thought she had retired from love. If you recognise your own behaviour here, there is advice in the exercise below.

LOWERING THE SHIELD

A shield might protect you from pain but it can keep out good things like love and affection.

- We are programmed to like and protect things that appear vulnerable: such as puppies and kittens. By contrast, something that appears invincible – such as a tank – does not provoke the same warm feelings.
- Picture your shield. What is it made of? Bricks or something that you can see through? How high is it? Up to your knees, your neck or over your head? How thick is it?
- Over the next few days, be aware of your shield and when it lowers and raises. How do you react under stress? How do other people react to your behaviour?

- With a clearer idea of your defences and how they operate, you are ready to make some changes. Next time that you feel threatened, take a deep breath or count to ten and then imagine lowering the shield a bit. Where do you see the shield now? What difference does this make to your behaviour?

- Think about what could help lower the shield further or make it more transparent. At work, for example, you could ask for help with a project, admit that you have a problem or simply buy time to think through all the implications and tackle them calmly.

- Remember, even small changes will pay dividends.

Ticking Clock Relationships

Do you feel that time is running out and that this is probably your last chance for happiness? This mindset will not only pile on the pressure but also make decision-making harder. Ticking clock relationships normally happen when a woman in her late thirties or early forties wants a baby or when both men and women in long-term relationships (possibly with children) feel that their relationship is going nowhere. They fear that time is running out and that they should look for a new relationship before they become too 'old and unattractive'.

Starting with the first scenario: 'I really wanted a baby but my boyfriend was younger and not ready,' explained Hannah, thirty-nine. 'Probably I held on much longer than I should have because it was obvious that he couldn't commit. We were together for five years and although we lived together at my place for most of the time, he always kept on another flat – even if it was just round the corner.'

'So what stopped you from confronting this issue?' I asked.

'He was very handsome – could have had anyone – and I didn't want to lose him, but mostly because I felt this was my last chance to have a baby. If I said goodbye to him, I was probably saying goodbye to becoming a mother too.'

Deep down, she had known for a while that this relationship was not good for her but had not been able to face all the implications of ending it. Carrying on might have seemed the best option at the time but Hannah's indecision seriously undermined her self-esteem.

While the ticking clock in the previous case was all too real, the urgency is normally all in the imagination. Howard, from the previous chapter, was considering splitting up so 'that there's time for us both to find someone who will truly love us.' Once he accepted that there was no real urgency, we were able to focus on changing his relationship not just with Natalie but with himself too. He started to face his own fears of getting older and unhappiness with the state of his career.

Having looked at some of the current circumstances that may be holding you back from making a decision, it is time to turn to events from the past that might be casting a shadow over today.

The Legacy of Divorce

If your parents divorced when you were a child, there will be two important long-term legacies. First, you will be determined not to make the same mistakes yourself but, second, you will be only too aware of the fleeting nature of love and find it harder to trust. As many people have said to me: 'If you don't marry, you don't get betrayed.' Alternatively, I have counselled people who have made hasty and ill-considered marriages – almost on the rebound of their parents' divorce – desperate for a little security. Unfortunately, these marriages have a divorce rate of twice the national average. Jeremy, the actor, is a good example of this phenomenon. His parents had a bitter divorce when he was ten and he got married himself at nineteen: 'My wife was twenty and also from a broken home. Of course, we weren't going to make the same mistakes, but we got divorced eight years ago when our sons were eleven and eight.'

Looking in further detail at the fallout from your parents' divorce, there are four potential scenarios which impact on your own relationships and make it harder to trust your own judgement.

1. Becoming a caregiver child

In many families divorce is such a traumatic experience that it leads to the partial or complete breakdown of parents' ability to care for their children. Normally this phase lasts for a few months but in others it will continue for years. In these cases, one of the children – normally the eldest – steps into the caregiver role.

A good example is Maggie, who is now in her late thirties. Her parents' marriage began to disintegrate in her early teens. She vividly remembers her father telling her of all the things he would have done 'if it wasn't for you'.

When she was sixteen and her father finally left, her mother became seriously depressed. 'On the good days, I'd come back from school and find that she'd spent the day staring at the wall. On the bad days, she'd be in tears. So I started taking her out and walking through the streets in the evening – anything to keep her moving. On winter evenings, when people had not yet closed the curtains, we would look in on all these lighted stages where normal people led normal lives.' When she had finished walking her mother around the town, Maggie would also fix tea for her younger sister and then start on her school work. At the weekend, she would help her mother with housework and shopping. Although she still saw her father, she felt alone and responsible. 'It would have seemed like betraying my mother if I'd told him what was really happening and, to be honest, I doubt he wanted to know,' she explained.

'So how did you cope?' I asked.

'I kept all my feelings in.'

'So who comforted you?'

For a second the confident outgoing woman who had worked all over the world was stripped away and I could see a lost child. 'My younger sister understood. I didn't have to say anything,' she finally replied. Maggie did not want to admit it, but the answer was nobody.

Bringing up children and running a house involves hundreds of choices. Before divorce, the parent with custody will have been used to talking any problems over with their partner. Suddenly they are on their own. Friends are helpful but are not there all the time. The result is that one of the children becomes the on-tap adviser and confidant/e of their mother or father. It is almost as though divorce has turned an adult into a helpless child and 'parentified' their son or daughter. It is not all bad news. The caregiving child gets immense pride from their exalted position in the household and in some cases, like in Maggie's, they can literally save their parent's sanity. However, forever sacrificing your own needs is not a good preparation for the give and take of successful adult relationships.

2. Troubled adolescence

Family is the scaffolding on which we climb through the different development stages – from helpless baby to independent adult. One of the most difficult times is adolescence where we start pushing against the rules set by our parents in order to forge our own values and identity.

If even the happiest families have trouble when the children hit adolescence, just imagine the problems for a divorced family. When parents live together, they can find a consensus on rules and standards of behaviour. However, this is harder when parents are struggling to be civil to each other. For intact families the children's adolescence takes centre stage – with both parents' full attention and steadying hand. Meanwhile, in a divorced family, the ongoing conflict between mother and father is centre stage. The result is either that their children's adolescence is put indefinitely on hold – as in the case of Maggie, who still has trouble separating from her mother – or happens in a dark corner unnoticed by anyone. For this reason, the children of divorced parents can reach adolescence earlier and with a lot of unresolved anger. In fact, research shows that the girls start experimenting with sex younger and both boys and girls have a higher use of alcohol and drugs than their peers.

'I started screwing boys when I was thirteen,' explained Alexis, thirty, whose parents divorced when she was ten, 'it made me feel wanted.' Unfortunately, she also got a reputation amongst her classmates. 'They called me "tramp" and the "class bike", so when I was offered cocaine I thought, "Everybody thinks I'm a bad girl, so why not?"' Not surprisingly, Alexis had no sense of direction and dropped out of university. She did various jobs and had several dead-end relationships, and from time to time her cocaine use became a problem. 'I would go home with men whom I wouldn't have looked at twice if I had not been off my face. Somehow I managed to keep it all together, but I had no idea what I was looking for. Even if I had known, I had no expectation of getting my needs met.'

3. Taking longer to become a fully formed adult

If the task of adolescence is breaking away from your home, becoming an adult is about discovering who you are, your personal standards and what you want from life, your job and your relationships.

Obviously this takes time but generally, somewhere between eighteen and twenty-three, most people develop a sense of their own identity. However, the children of divorce are often too frightened to experiment and instead of actively choosing someone, just drift into the first relationship offered.

'I met Sam during my first week at university; we shared a kitchen and soon a bed. Don't get me wrong, he's nice but he's very shy and relies on me a lot,' explains Lauren who is twenty-five and still with Sam. 'You see, we both found moving away from home a bit of a wrench – so we leaned on each other. But while I made friends and enjoyed the experience, Sam withdrew into himself.' They have almost split up on numerous occasions but Lauren has always stopped short. 'He starts to cry and I cave in. You see, I know the pain of being left. I can still remember what my father was wearing, the leather case with the grease stain, and how my sister tried to bar the way. I couldn't do that to someone else.' It is almost as if some children of divorce do not have the confidence to judge a relationship. Instead of actively seeking the right relationship, they take what is on offer.

Young women whose parents divorced often choose an older man, rather than experimenting with men of their own age. The older man seems appealing for a number of reasons – beyond replacing the father figure lost through divorce. First, older men are less likely to cheat on a younger woman – and all children of divorce fear betrayal almost as much as they long for love. Second, older men are happy to stay at home in the evening and therefore avoid arousing feelings of jealousy. Third, they have already discovered who they are and what they want; this is very appealing to someone who is uncertain about their own identity.

A typical example was Jonathan, who was forty-eight, and his partner, Leah, who was twenty-eight when they came into counselling, but they had been together since she was twenty. 'The age difference was not a problem at the beginning of the relationship. She was very mature and I found that we wanted the same things,' explained Jonathan. 'We even have similar tastes in music and he took me to Elton John, Joe Cocker and Tina Turner concerts,' added Leah, describing the start of their relationship. 'We also liked nights in front of the television and entertaining at home.' I had a picture of an almost scarily mature girl and then it struck me: rather than the usual method of trial and error to discover her identity, Leah had simply adopted Jonathan's. No wonder they had similar tastes! However, eight years on, Leah had reached twenty-eight and had begun to feel trapped. 'It's like he's stifling me, forever telling me what to do,' she complained. 'But I see you about to do something stupid – like arguing with the boss at work – and I want to step in and stop you,' Jonathan replied. 'But I've got to make my own mistakes,' said Leah. She had started her own journey into being an adult.

4. Overly self-reliant

Divorce can have some positive benefits. Not only do the adults stuck in a loveless marriage get a second chance, but also their children can learn some important lessons – for example, the need to be self-reliant. Maggie, the caregiver child whom we met earlier in this chapter, became the first person in her family to go to university and she has become well known within her chosen career. 'I want to make my mark and do something good,' she explained. 'It's a great time to be a woman and I want to make the most of it. If love happens on the way, all well and good. However, I won't be looking for it.'

Underneath the professional confidence is a huge fear of being out of control in her personal relationships. She has protected herself by having first one relationship and then another with men who she knew would never commit. 'I'm terrified the relationship is not going to be mutual – any hint that he's losing interest and I'll end it,' she explained. She also told a sad story about visiting a country where she used to work and catching up with an ex-lover. He was now married 'with a beautiful wife and an adorable baby'. However, she was quick to point out that the ex-boyfriend had made a pass at her on the trip back to the airport. 'So you see, I wasn't jealous of her,' Maggie finished. The fear of repeating her parents' mistakes had translated into a fear of commitment.

The children of divorce believe very strongly in love but they expect to be betrayed. Sadly, the very thing that they want the most and the thing that they fear the most are the same thing.

ARE YOU READY TO LOVE?

This quiz is divided into three parts. Part one is for someone in a new or emerging relationship. Part two is for someone questioning a long-term relationship. Part three is for everybody:

Part one:

1. Are you still in love with an ex-partner?
2. Do you feel resentment or rage towards an ex-partner?
3. Do you have unanswered questions about why your last relationship ended?

Part two:

4. Has someone at work or a friend become increasingly important to your happiness?
5. Do you fantasise about how life might be if somehow you could be together?
6. Have you been confiding in a friend complaints about your partner that you would not/could not discuss with him or her?

Part three:

7. Do you dislike yourself?
8. Do you worry that if someone knew the real you they would probably not want to be in a relationship with you?
9. Are you closed off and do you keep people at a distance?

Interpreting your answers:

Part one: If you answered yes to either question one or two, you are not ready to love again. Although resentment or rage might seem to help you distance yourself from the past, it can encourage dating to make your ex jealous, dating for revenge against your ex, or dating to prove that you are still attractive. These are not good foundations for a relationship. If you answered yes to question three, there could be some unfinished business with your ex that needs sorting out before you are ready to commit.

Part two: These questions test whether you are at risk of having an inappropriate friendship or an emotional affair. Question six looks at whether you are talking to your friends about your problems (and building up a head of resentment) rather than your partner (and doing something about them). If you are tempted by another man or woman, step back before it turns into a full-blown affair and deepens the problems in your relationship.

Part three: These questions are about your self-image. When you don't have good self-esteem, you are vulnerable to people who take advantage. Alternatively, when genuine love is offered, you can find it hard to accept – worrying that if someone likes you there must be something wrong with them. If this sounds familiar, boost your self-esteem with another book in this series: *Learn to Love Yourself Enough*.

Overall: If you answered 'no' or 'not really' to all your questions, congratulations: you are ready to love.

Do As You Would Be Done By

In the name of finding love, our behaviour is often anything but loving. We frequently judge on the most superficial grounds, condemn whole tranches of the population and lie or bend the truth. However, we expect others to consider our character and personality, not just our looks, weight and bank balance. Moreover, we demand honesty and transparency. In effect, there is one rule for us and one rule for everybody else. How can love – which thrives on equality – stand a chance?

In committed relationships, we excuse our bad behaviour on the grounds that we are tired, stressed or preoccupied. However, we are not always willing to offer the same consideration to our partner and often put things we dislike down not to an isolated event (therefore trifling and transitory) but to character flaws (therefore serious and permanent).

This is why the third step to achieving clarity draws on ancient wisdom: 'Do unto others as you would have them do unto you' (the Bible, Matthew 7:12; Luke 6:31), or 'What you do not wish upon yourself, extend not to others' (Confucius, Chinese philosopher, 551–479 BC), and 'This is the sum of duty; do naught unto others what you would not have them do unto you' (Mahabharata, ancient Sanskrit text of Hindu mythology and philosophy). The following exercise puts this idea into action.

LOOKING IN THE MIRROR

When people complain about their partner – he never listens, she runs me down – they are often guilty of the very same thing themselves! So phrases like 'single men are losers' or 'single women in their thirties are bitter' tell us as much, if not more, about the person complaining as about their targets. This is because relationships are like mirrors; we see the things we don't like about ourselves in the behaviour of others. Except, rather than admit to our own failings or cutting our nearest and dearest a bit of slack, we find it easier to rail against others.

So without stopping to think, write down your three main criticisms about the men or women that you have dated or the singles scene in general. If you are in a committed relationship, write down your three biggest complaints about your partner.

1. ....

2. ....

3. ....

Now imagine looking in the mirror. Could any of those criticisms be levelled at you? Even in a small way? If so, what changes could you make? Try being more understanding towards your partner or new lover's foibles because forgiving others is the first step to forgiving ourselves.

Summing Up

When facing a relationship turning point, it is often easier to see the failings of our partner rather than face up to our own contribution to the problem. So take a good look at your lifestyle and your past relationships, and the effect these might be having on your current crisis. Often our strategies for coping with underlying long-term problems have the unexpected side effect of making matters worse rather than better. Although it might be painful to face problems head-on, tackling them provides a way forward.

IN A NUTSHELL:

- Instead of getting frustrated trying to change your partner's behaviour, concentrate on what you can more readily change: yourself.

- Often what holds us back from making a choice is our fear of the consequences. Ask yourself: How real are my fears? Could stepping round them be making the situation worse?

- Commit to change by setting a concrete goal – something to measure your progress against. How could you take the first step and launch this journey?

STEP 4

UNDERSTANDING INTIMACY

Humans are social creatures. We have an almost animal need to pair off, which friendship, however good, just cannot satisfy. A loving, sensual and sexual relationship is the best refuge when the going gets tough, a springboard to personal growth and a source of strength which improves our overall health. In an era of short-term business contracts, fears about personal safety and rapid technological change, we need the reassurance that a loving relationship provides. So everybody should be in favour of intimacy and being able to rely on another human being, but it's not that straightforward. That's why my fourth question is:

How do you feel about commitment?

Although at first sight this question might seem more for people looking for love rather than those in settled relationships, I find everybody – to a greater or lesser extent – gets caught up in this issue.

How to be Comfortable with Commitment

When I talk about the need to embrace commitment, many of my single clients become angry. Mia, thirty-two, is typical: 'I have no problem with commitment whatsoever. I'm ready to settle down. It's the men out there. They're all committed commitmentphobes.' When I looked at Mia's relationship history, she had indeed thrown herself into several relationships. The most recent was with someone she had met through work. 'We started off arguing all the time – because we had fundamentally different attitudes to everything – but this developed into a strong attraction. I started enjoying his company and he told me about his unhappy relationship.'

They soon started a passionate affair and every time he was in town, Mia would drop everything and make time for him. She stopped seeing other guys and would write to him several times a week. 'He emails back occasionally. The most recent email was a complaint about his girlfriend. I tell him we'd be so good together – I'd marry him in a shot – but he seems frightened of making a lasting commitment. How long can I hold on? I need some sort of sign.'

On the one hand, Mia appears comfortable with commitment, but on the other she has chosen someone who lives in another country (and visits her town only three or four times a year), who is already in another relationship and, on her own admission, holds different beliefs. It does not seem a recipe for success. So what is really happening here?

When I first started training as a marital thera-pist, I tended to take my clients' words at face value. However, I was working with a man who kept saying how much he valued his freedom, how he didn't love his wife, how he couldn't stand living with her any more. I will always remember the wisdom of my supervisor. She interrupted my report on the case: 'How long has he been coming to counselling?'

'Five weeks,' I told her.

'His mouth might say he doesn't want to save the relationship, but week after week his legs bring him up two flights of stairs to your office,' she explained. From that moment on, I started listening to my client's legs rather than his lips, challenged his desire to leave, and the couple eventually solved their differences. I share this story because lots of singles talk about being ready for commitment but end up sabotaging their prospects in one of two ways. I call these 'blowing hot and cold' and 'being over-committed'.

Blowing Hot and Cold

Everyone has used this strategy at some point in their life – especially when young or inexperienced and finding themselves too deep in a relationship too quickly. However, you should be concerned if you recognise a repeating pattern or if this description fits your most recent relationship.

- At the very beginning, it feels safe to blow red-hot as you are still trying to win over the other person, or because there is some sort of safety net. For example, falling for someone on holiday or someone about to leave the country.

- As the relationship continues, you give off all the right signals about commitment and, at the time, probably mean them. However, the day-to-day reality of being in a relationship leaves you feeling hemmed in, overwhelmed and wanting to pull back.

- You begin to pull away and become frosty.

- Once in the coldest part of this cycle, even reasonable requests for intimacy feel like demands and need to be resisted. At this point, you will value 'space' and 'time for myself'.

- In the worst cases, the fear can turn into panic attacks and you literally feel the need to flee.

- More often, you will erect artificial barriers to intimacy. For example, turning off your mobile, not returning phone calls or being unwilling to plan into the future as this is perceived as 'putting pressure on'. Instead, you stress the advantages of being 'spontaneous'.

- Sometimes the barriers are physical. For example, taking a job assignment in another city. In other cases, the barriers come from another relationship. These might be socially acceptable – like problems with childcare from a first marriage or caring for an elderly relative. However, more often, people who blow hot and cold run more than one sexual relationship at the same time.

- Nostalgia for past relationships can be a strong factor too. In comparison with your feelings about your current boyfriend or girlfriend, issues with your ex seem insignificant. This old relationship is stone-cold dead, and therefore it is safe to blow hot with your ex again.

- If there is too much distance, too many barriers or the other person shows signs of leaving the relationship, your approach will change. What you are about to lose increases in value and therefore you start to turn up the heat again.

- The other person feels positive and he or she becomes committed again. The courtship tips back into the hot phase. Although you promise 'This time it will be different', nothing has fundamentally changed.

- The whole cycle will repeat again and again – sometimes for years on end.

These 'blowing hot and cold' relationships normally end bitterly – although it tends to be your partner who suffers the most. Sometimes, there are so many barriers and excuses that the relationship simply ceases to exist. In other cases, you simply disappear or meet someone else who, at the time, seems the perfect partner.

In effect, this kind of relationship is like a dance – with the distance between the two partners carefully maintained. If your partner steps forward, you step back. When they retreat, you move forward again.

COPING WITH RELATIONSHIP ANXIETY ATTACKS

If you recognise yourself as someone who blows hot and cold, the following steps will help break the dance:

1. Accept that relationships can be scary and that everybody feels like this from time to time.
2. Look at your past to understand where your fears come from. Perhaps your parents got divorced or there was a painful early romance? What patterns has your childhood set up and how do they influence your behaviour today?

3. Understand that the best way to deal with fear is to confront it. The more that you shy away from something the more the fear grows.

4. Explain to your partner what circumstances throw up shadows from the past. In this way he or she will know when to tread carefully.

5. Keep a fear diary. Write down when you feel uncomfortable down one side of the page and provide a rational explanation on the other. For example: Fear = 'he's late, he doesn't love me'. Rational explanation = 'traffic's bad'. Writing fears down stops them multiplying in your head and accesses the adult logical part of your personality.

Rebalance your life. Draw a pie chart which shows how you divide your time and energy between: relationship, work, friends, myself. Next, draw a second chart showing how you would like it to be. How can you make this future happen?

Being Over-committed

This is the hardest of the dances to self-diagnose; after all, it is easier to listen to our lips than to examine the more subtle messages from our behaviour. So read the following questions with an open mind.

- Would you describe yourself as very romantic and someone who often makes big gestures – like turning up unannounced in a faraway city?

- Do you fall in love very quickly and commit yourself without really knowing someone or giving them a chance to prove that they are truly worthy of your devotion?

- What is your reaction to negative information about someone? Do you tend to minimise it? For example: He's married – that could change. She flirts with everyone – it doesn't matter, she's going to be mine.

- Have you fallen for men or women who were unavailable, seldom available or made themselves unavailable using the techniques outlined in 'blowing hot and cold'?

- Looking back at past relationships, did you know about the problems but believed that either you could cope ('It doesn't matter, I don't need that much attention') or you could easily change the other person ('He just needs to get more in touch with his feelings' or 'She just needs to believe in herself')?

- Do you make yourself totally available to your beloved – right from the start? By this I mean physically, emotionally and sexually.
- When you become more emotional and open, have you ever found that your beloved becomes more distant?
- Do your boundaries come down in direct proportion to the barriers put up by the other person?
- If you totalled up the hours spent on your last relationship, would you have spent longer talking about your beloved with friends, thinking about him/her or doing activities that linked you to your beloved (listening to their favourite music or writing poetry) than actual face-to-face time with him/her?
- Have you thought that a relationship could be better if only . . . (put in your personal idea)? This normally involves spending quality time together – for example, a romantic holiday – with all your energy going into making this happen. If you have managed to pull off one of these special events, did it make that much difference in the long term?
- When a relationship ends, do you take a disproportionately long time to recover?

- Can you find yourself still holding a candle for someone, even years later?

Most people will have answered yes to one, maybe two of these questions, but if you found yourself nodding as you went down the list it probably means that you favour this kind of dance. In therapy, people who are 'over-committed' discover that they were more attached to a fantasy version of their beloved than the real person they dated. This was certainly the case for Mia whose beloved was already involved with somebody else: 'I didn't really love him, but what I thought he could be.' In effect, she had been projecting her dreams on to him. Once she realised that she had been mourning not for what she had lost but for some fantasy of how it might have been, she found it easier to move on.

The Combination Effect

Sometimes people use both of the dances that avoid true commitment. Jackie, who is now twenty-nine, met Rob in her mid-twenties on a holiday in Greece. In this relationship, she blew 'hot and cold'. The attraction was instant and the couple spent twenty-four hours together non-stop: 'We did all that goofy stuff like building a sandcastle together on the beach, champagne picnics, and we stayed up the whole night cuddling and kissing. But all too soon, his boat had to leave the island where I was staying. It was the perfect holiday romance.'

Although they exchanged addresses, Jackie did not really expect a relationship. 'He lived in New York and I had a demanding job. However, we started writing and telephoning, and he suggested flying over to visit. I was very flattered and being reunited at the airport was like something out of a movie. I was on such a high but it did not stop me noticing that he was a couple of inches shorter than I had remembered. He had expected me to live in a thatched cottage rather than a small one-bedroom flat, but we had a great time. It was strange to have him under my feet for a week, having to entertain him all the time, and, as I still had to work, it was exhausting. Don't get me wrong, I was dreading him leaving but looking forward to doing what I wanted again.'

There were also times when Jackie wanted a bit of private space. 'I would suggest that he took a bath, so that I could catch up on a report for work, but he'd keep calling for me to come and scrub his back.' Rob was ten years older than Jackie and had inherited a lot of money from his parents, so was in the position to make grand gestures. 'When, on our last night together, he suggested a cruise around the Caribbean – all expenses paid – I wanted to put the brakes on. It was all moving too quickly and I didn't like the idea of "being bought", so I thanked him but declined.'

Despite her reservations, the relationship continued for another two years. Jackie paid for her own trip to New York and Rob came back to the United Kingdom on a couple of occasions. However, Jackie kept on being ambivalent about making a commitment. At one moment she would be on a high: 'On my first trip to the States, I tried to sit as close to the front of the plane as possible. Somehow I thought that would get me that little bit nearer to Rob's arms again.' The next, she was feeling hemmed in and hiding behind work commitments. When Rob was not around, Jackie would miss him and send out all the signs that she wanted the relationship. When he was there, she was not so sure. 'It was hard for Rob when I turned chilly. He'd be all concerned and ask if anything was the matter. I wanted to scream: "Leave me alone."'

In her next relationship, Jackie became 'over-committed'. On this occasion, she managed to avoid all her old feelings of being trapped or hemmed in and threw herself wholeheartedly into the relationship. So how did she overcome her fears? This is the sad part: she didn't. She chose someone who was not truly available. Jake lived only an hour's drive away. The sex was incredible. There was only *one* problem: Jake's profession. He was a dog breeder with rows and rows of runs in his back garden. The dogs provided endless excuses for his not seeing Jackie: a bitch would be about to give birth, staff shortages meant Jake had to work extra shifts, he had visits from prospective owners or he was too busy hand-rearing a pup that had been rejected by its mother. Jackie explained how Jake would put up other barriers: 'He'd never want to make another date straight away. It would be a couple of days before I'd catch him in or he'd call back – so there was never any continuity. I kept thinking it would all be great if we could spend some proper time together. I tried to get him to come to my birthday weekend and meet all my friends – but on the Saturday afternoon he had last-minute problems and I lost my temper. So he opted out not only of the party but also of coming down for Sunday lunch with my mum and sister.'

However, it was not all bad and the relationship lasted for three years. 'He was a really caring guy. Lots of insight and well read, too. He introduced me to some great books and music. If only he could have met me halfway.' Unfortunately, Jackie had been keeping the relationship alive by sheer force of will. (She had even persuaded her best friend to buy one of Jake's pups, so that she could let him see what 'fun' her friends were and integrate him further into her life.) Certainly, Jackie had been committed, but to a man who showed no sign of committing himself – or indeed fulfilling quite a lot of the basic requirements of a true relationship. In effect, the commitment had been all on Jackie's part.

It took several weeks of counselling before Jackie could understand that although she wanted intimacy, she was equally frightened of getting it. Instead of facing up to this dilemma, she had been involved in a complicated dance around the problem. With her lips, she had been all for a relationship, but her choice of men had stopped her from having to deal with the reality. In a sense, she had had her cake but did not have to eat it!

SMALL STEPS TOWARDS FEELING OK ABOUT COMMITMENT

1. **Accept where you are starting from.** Our culture places a lot of stress on freedom, independence and pleasing yourself. The news is full of theft and violence and so it is harder than ever before to trust people. However, we make it worse by pointing the finger at ex-partners rather than accepting our own commitment issues. If you recognised yourself – even if only in a mild form – in either 'blowing hot and cold' or 'being over-committed', congratulate yourself. Owning up to a problem is halfway to solving it.

2. **Aim for small changes.** Once people accept that a certain type of person is bad for them, the temptation is to go for the complete opposite. For example, Jackie felt under pressure from Rob flying in from New York, so decided to choose someone who would be laid-back like Jake. However, the dynamic of the relationship was the same – commitment problems – she just played the opposite role. Think of commitment as a continuum with a hermit at one end and someone who brings a removal van on the second date at the other.

Instead of flying to the far end – which will freak you out and probably be too far in the other direction – aim to move a little more into the middle.

3. **Be up-front.** I advocate what I call 'Showing the Owner's Manual'. After a couple of dates, mention your particular pattern. This does not have to be a big conversation; ideally it should be over in a couple of sentences. After all, you are just showing the manual – not trying to sell! For example, 'I just thought I'd warn you that I like you, but sometimes I can come on a bit strong. So please tell me if I start moving too quickly.' Alternatively: 'I'm really enjoying going out with you, but I thought I should make you aware that I have had some bad experiences in the past. So if I seem to hold back, let me know and I'll tell you if it is just my natural reserve or whether I feel things are going too fast.' Remember this is not a confession, a detailed explanation or a relationship history. You are making the other person aware of your issues, but, more importantly, are giving them permission to ask questions in the future. So instead of making assumptions, they will check out their impressions.

4. **Monitor your progress.** Our attitude to intimacy is deeply ingrained, so do not expect too much too soon. However, you will be amazed at how much better it feels even just a few steps further towards the centre of the scale. You can start with friends – where the stakes are lower – so if you have blown hot and cold, ask a friend to come and stay. If you previously felt that your space was invaded after twenty-four hours – aim for thirty-six. If you are over-committed (and tend to be clinging), you could try lengthening the time between calls to your best friend. You might find, once given the opportunity, that he or she will initiate more calls.

5. **Find a level of intimacy which feels comfortable for you.** I have met couples who have vowed never to spend a night apart and I know others who would go crazy without business trips or occasional weekends away with mates. Each couple needs to find what works for them.

6. **Keep the lines of communication open.** Never underestimate how confessing to a feeling can release the tension. For many people, this is the single most important way

to cut down their fears. James, forty, and Emma, thirty, hit a barrier early in their relationship. 'I felt completely overloaded. I had a difficult patch where I had to fight for every freelance contract,' explains James. 'At the same time, I felt I was expected to help boost Emma's career and be her mentor too. I remember walking through Leicester Square on a sunny afternoon and there were all these people enjoying themselves. They seemed to be without a care in the world. I knew I could cope with my own problems but not Emma's too. One thing led to another and I sank lower and lower, until I started questioning whether we should even be together.' Fortunately, they communicated well: Emma noticed that James had turned sullen and James was honest about his feelings. 'I don't think I can sort out your career and keep my own on track. I just don't have the energy,' he told her. Emma was furious and hurt: 'What makes you think I'm asking?' In effect, James had assumed wrongly – in this case – that he was Emma's full-time cheerleader. Although the couple had a nasty argument they had learned a lot about each other. Often our new love's needs, expectations and demands for commitment exist only in our own fevered imagination. The only way to discover the truth is to be open and talk.

So Why Do People Fall Into This Pit?

Human beings have two basic but contradictory needs: intimacy and independence. We are social creatures and need the emotional and physical support that comes from a loving relationship – whether from a partner, friend or parent. However, we also value our autonomy and need enough freedom to be ourselves – rather than be crushed by the expectations of other people. It is a hard balancing trick: if you are too independent, you have no relationship; too much intimacy and you lose your personal sense of identity.

In successful relationships, both partners are responsible for some of the intimacy and some of the independence. However, under stress, people get polarised and one partner will push for more time together and the other will retreat into their work, watching television, working or playing on the computer, going to the pub or taking up an all-consuming hobby.

Psychologists believe our response to intimacy is based on our childhood experiences. People who had a 'good enough' childhood will find it easy to get close to someone else (secure attachment) but not feel that their sense of themselves is at risk. They make up 56 per cent of the population.

Meanwhile, people who had 'bad' childhood experiences will find it hard to trust other people (avoidant attachment). Not surprisingly, they prefer to keep people at arm's length. In a mild form, it involves guarding personal time inside a relationship. In the middle and more extreme forms, it either means becoming a loner or more likely – because intimacy is a basic human need – swinging back and forth between intimacy and independence (in other words blowing hot and cold).

Twenty-five per cent of the population have some degree of avoidant attachment. When I talked about commitment with Jeremy, the actor, he immediately recognised himself. 'I even pushed my wife away from time to time but she was quite self-contained. She didn't really need me, so the relationship never felt too intimate.' So how did he feel about intimacy? 'It's like I'm going to be swallowed up and I worry when I enter a new relationship. It's like diving into a swimming pool and not knowing where the edges are – very painful.' Although intimacy frightened Jeremy, he had a strong need to be in a committed relationship (probably the fallout from his parents' divorce) so he had been using either a strong physical attraction or finding a 'soul partner' to overcome his fears and launch into a relationship. However, the real issues had not gone away and all his relationships had ended after about nine months.

The third category is people who felt unfulfilled as children and as adults can never get enough love. This is called anxious attachment. These people worry because their partners seem reluctant to get as close as they would wish. In the mild form, this is the half of the relationship pushing for more time together. In the middle, it is someone who dismisses their own needs and puts everything into the relationship. At the far end, this becomes 'being over-committed'. This category has 19 per cent of the population. So where do you fit in? Look at the quiz on attachment styles in relationships, work and social situations.

WHAT IS YOUR ATTACHMENT STYLE?

This quiz highlights the differences between the attachment styles, offers insights into how other people approach the same issues, and offers some targeted advice for your personal style.

1. How do you feel about your work and your colleagues?
   a) I am satisfied with colleagues and the level of job security.
   b) I do not feel truly appreciated by my colleagues and feel that I deserve promotion.
   c) My colleagues are lazy and some of them not very good at their jobs but I feel that my job is secure.

2. Which of the following best describes your work pattern?
   a) I can work well both alone and as part of a team.
   b) I prefer working with other people and get them involved in my tasks.
   c) I work best alone.

3. What is your work/life balance like?
   a) I get pleasure from both my relationships and my work.

b) Problems with my love life sometimes interfere with my work.

c) My work life is more important than my love life.

4. You have a new work colleague who, within hours of arriving, has told you all sorts of personal information. How do you react?

a) I like people who are up-front but I would not respond in a similar manner until I got to know the new colleague better.

b) I like people who self-disclose and I would respond by telling him/her everything about myself too.

c) I do not like people who behave like this and would never dream of telling work colleagues such private information.

5. Which of the following statements best describes your feelings about yourself?

a) Although I have my bad days, I generally have fairly good self-esteem.

b) I have low self-esteem and can never get enough compliments.

c) People see me as confident and in control but they would think differently if they saw the real me.

Mostly a): Secure attachment
You are generally comfortable being close to other people and have few issues about trust. Congratulations, you are well placed for the next part of the programme.

Breakthrough tip: If you did not answer a) on all the questions, look at whether you were more likely to answer b) or c) on the rest and read this section too.

Mostly b): Anxious attachment
Being close to other people is a very attractive proposition for you, but some people find that you come on too strong. You have a tendency to disclose lots of information about yourself and later wonder if it was a good thing. When it comes to intimate relationships, you find that you can never get as close as you wish and worry about the other person betraying you. In the past, you have often become too committed too soon and got your fingers burnt. The result is that you can try too hard or, worse, imagine slights when none were intended.

Breakthrough tip: Look before you leap and really weigh up if someone is truly worthy of your love or interested in your friendship. Next time you catch yourself about to commit, step back and observe. See if you can double the time you normally take to fall for someone or decide to become friends. Even slowing up a bit will help improve your judgement.

Mostly c): Avoidant attachment

You find it difficult to trust other people or to allow yourself to depend on them. You are nervous when someone gets too close and often your partners want more closeness than you feel comfortable with. In past relationships, you have blown hot and cold. This is because one half of you really wants to be in a loving relationship, but the other half is rather scared.

Breakthrough tip: Be wary of the messages that you give out during the first stages of a new relationship. A heady combination of lust, the excitement of the new and the hope that it will work this time make you appear more committed than you truly feel. Try not to set up patterns that will end with you feeling cornered again. For example, if you phone every day, the other person will expect and come to rely on frequent contact. So keep asking yourself: Am I writing cheques that I might not be able to honour?

Summing Up

It is often easier to talk the talk of commitment than to follow through and commit. One way to deal with this contradiction is to blow hot and cold about the relationship (and to blame our partner for making us behave in this manner) or to become over-committed to someone who does not truly return our feelings (and blame them for the lack of commitment).

IN A NUTSHELL:

- Beyond the first heady moments of falling in love, no couple wants to be together constantly. So build breaks and time apart into your general routine.
- If your partner asking for time apart makes you anxious, cultivate a positive voice inside your head: 'It doesn't mean that he's fallen out of love' or 'She will be back soon if I don't push her away by being clingy.'
- Talk about your fears with your partner. It is the most effective way of cutting them down to size.

STEP 5

GET THE
TIMING RIGHT

So far in the journey from limbo to certainty, you have checked whether you have fallen for one of the myths about love which put unnecessary pressure on relationships. You have taken a dispassionate look at both your partner and yourself, and discovered whether hidden fears are sabotaging your commitment to each other. However, there is another ingredient for making relationships work: getting the timing right.

It is perfectly possible to meet the right person but to push for commitment too early and frighten him or her off. Conversely, some couples put off making a proper commitment – like living together, getting married or starting a family – for too long and the relationship goes off the boil. Sometimes you and your partner can be at different life stages and this can put a huge amount of pressure on your bond. So here's my fifth question:

Is this the right time?

You have been out together on a few occasions and everything seems promising. But how can you tell if this is 'just friends' or the makings of a life-long love affair?

Fortunately, there is scientific research into just this question, plus useful work on the honeymoon period of love and the natural rhythm of relationships. This knowledge will not only help you progress at the right pace but decide if this new man or woman is the right person for you. Later in the chapter, I will explain the landmarks in settled relationships and how some problems have their roots in the disruption of moving from one phase to another.

The First Steps Into Making a Relationship

There are three types of outings or dates: *Getting to know you* (assessing if there is any connection), *Fun outings* (enjoying each other's company and checking compatibility) and, finally, *Courting* (the beginnings of a lasting relationship). It is impossible to get to the third type of outing without moving through the first two. Unfortunately, many potential relationships are crushed because one half is in too much of a hurry to court. 'I just like to know where I stand,' says Ingrid, who is thirty-two. 'I haven't got time to waste with men who are not interested in a commitment.' When I ask how she can judge, she becomes a little coy, but after some probing admits: 'I will float the subject of marriage; perhaps a friend has got engaged and I will see how he reacts. Although I'd never ask directly for his opinions on marriage.' It might seem casual to the person dropping the 'M' word, but seldom comes across this way.

Jerome is also in his thirties and rarely sees anyone past the third or fourth date. 'I sometimes think that women are obsessed with commitment. Sure, I want to settle down, have children – the whole nine yards – but I want it to be with someone who loves me, not with a woman who seems desperate to commit to – if I am being brutally honest – almost anyone,' Jerome explains. 'I can practically time when the conversation will turn to settling down, marriage, babies or whatever. It is such a turn-off. I'm still getting to know her and she's measuring me for a morning suit.' On one occasion, he was really keen on a girl whom he had met at work. They had been out the night before, and when he arrived at the office Jerome was thinking of calling her. 'I sat down and logged on for my emails and found that I had two from her. She had also left a message on my voicemail; I still was thinking of calling when the phone rang. She wanted to meet me in the third-floor lobby – straightaway. When I arrived she shoved a piece of paper into my hand and disappeared. It was a poem dedicated "to my soulmate".'

Obviously the time needed to progress from 'getting to know you' to 'courting' will change from couple to couple, but, as a rule of thumb, it is somewhere between five and ten outings.

The Three Months Test

On the one hand, trying to define a relationship too soon is like pulling up a plant cutting and checking whether it is growing roots; but on the other, just wishing and hoping for the best can lead to a dead-end relationship. Margi, thirty-two, has been with her boyfriend for three years. 'He had a nasty divorce and his motto is "once bitten, twice shy". I understand about the marriage thing, but he won't even promise we'll be together for ever. I catch myself telling friends that "marriage isn't all it's cracked up to be" but sometimes I think that the only person I'm fooling is myself. Part of me thinks "I deserve to be with someone who wants the same things", but I love him and we've had a lot of good times together. Why throw that all away?'

Although one of my central messages is 'Don't judge too quickly', the moment of truth cannot be put off indefinitely. In my opinion, three months is an important milestone. How does your relationship measure up?

- Have you both stopped accepting 'dates' from other people?
- Can you openly label each other as boyfriend or girlfriend?
- Does conversation flow like wine?
- Can you relax in each other's presence?
- Do you *like* yourself when you are with your new man or woman?
- Are you both interested in the particulars of each other's lives?

- Who is putting the most energy into developing the relationship? Who calls? Who suggests outings?
- If it seems that you are doing the majority of the work, step back and give him or her room to take the initiative. Sometimes it is better to let a relationship fold than put increasing amounts of energy into preserving it.
- If your partner has been making most of the running, what happens if you let down your defences and suggest something that progresses the relationship? For example, meeting family or taking a short break together.

What About Love?

A book about deciding whether a relationship has a future would not be complete without a proper discussion about love and how it influences our behaviour. Unfortunately, few of the founding fathers of psychology have examined love. However, there is one honourable exception. Starting in the mid-sixties, experimental psychologist Dorothy Tennov set out to try and understand how falling in love could be the source of both supreme joy and intense misery.

She undertook five hundred in-depth interviews and discovered that men and women, from all cultures, described the experience in the same way. Despite the obstacles to overcome and the fear of love being unrequited, 95 per cent of her respondents still called love 'a beautiful experience'. Eighty-three per cent felt that 'anyone who has never been in love is missing one of life's most pleasurable experiences'. Forty-two per cent described it as 'living on top of a cloud'. To differentiate between the magic of falling in love and the settled, everyday love of a long-term couple, Tennov coined the word 'limerence' (*Love and Limerence*, Stein & Day, 1980).

IS IT LOVE OR IS IT LIMERENCE?

Although romantic novelists, poets and song-writers talk about love, really they are describing limerence. As we will see, there are some key differences between love and limerence:

- Under the spell of limerence, everything about our beloved is special. Tennov quotes one of her respondents: 'Anything that she liked, I liked; anything that belonged to her acquired a certain magic – her handbag, her notebook, her pencil. I abhor the sight of toothmarks on a pencil; they disgust me. But not her toothmarks. Hers were sacred; her wonderful mouth had been there.' In a long-term relationship, the pencil covered in toothmarks would probably end up in the bin rather than being the centrepiece of a shrine.

- Despite the power of limerence to infuse everything with a romantic glow, two-thirds of men and three-quarters of women could identify their partner's character defects or bad habits. However, these problems are happily overlooked or downplayed. Tennov quotes one respondent: 'Yes, I knew he gambled, I knew he sometimes drank too much, and I knew he did not read a book from one year to the next. I knew it, but I didn't incorporate it into the overall image. I dwelt on his wavy hair, the way he looked at me, the thought of him driving me to work in the morning.' These feelings are very different from those experienced by established couples for whom wavy hair does not trump coming home drunk.

- Under the spell of limerence, it is impossible to stop thinking about your beloved. In extreme cases, students drop out of courses and we all know work colleagues who get nothing done because they are either daydreaming about their beloved, writing sexy emails or chatting on the phone. By contrast, married couples are perfectly capable of working, running a house, and enjoying a social life both independently and together.

- It impossible to be limerent with more than one person at a time or even to have eyes for anyone but your beloved. 'I went to a friend's stag weekend and we ended up in a lap-dancing club,' explains William, twenty-eight. 'There were some pretty girls and all my friends were catcalling and laughing. I could accept that one girl, for example, had nice legs, but I judged them too long and her ankles were ugly. I just kept comparing every girl unfavourably with Holly.' By contrast, 90 per cent of established couples regularly fantasise about someone else during lovemaking.

- Most powerful of all, limerence makes us feel that we can cope with anything. Financial difficulties fade into the background. So what if our job is boring or our mother domineering? Hand in hand with our beloved, we can conquer the world; obstacles are something to embrace: an opportunity to prove or strengthen our feelings for one another.

The Problem With Limerence

Limerence is a heady, almost addictive force. There is just *one* problem. It does not last for ever. At the bottom end of the scale, full-blown limerence lasts for about six months. This is normally when the love has not been returned. A good example is Owen, forty-eight, who fell for a much younger colleague: 'Her look when we passed each other in the corridor would send me into ecstasy: perhaps she felt the same way too. I longed for her so intensely that the only relief was fantasising about a possible life together: sharing croissants and coffee in a long garden that leads down to the river or touring the churches and galleries of Venice together. However, the relief was just momentary because my fantasies made me long for her even more.' Unfortunately, his colleague was engaged to someone else and Owen had enough of a grip on reality to know that she would probably not enjoy visiting galleries anyway. Even though Owen's colleague remained oblivious, his limerent feelings remained strong. Fortunately, they did burn themselves out after a while.

Limerence is even more of a problem when it has crystallised for one half of a couple in a short-term relationship but the other half has drifted away. 'It really was the perfect love,' moans Ryan, twenty-eight. 'We were both mature students at university, had tons in common and spent all our spare time together. We would work side by side in the library, so we knew if the other was going to the coffee shop and could coordinate our breaks. We were real soulmates; I thought we'd spend the rest of our lives together.' Their break-up came as a shock to Ryan: 'I hadn't seen it coming. In retrospect, she had been studying alone more and more – but I thought it was because exams were looming – and then she had to go home for the weekend. At the time, I put it down to her missing her mum.'

Unfortunately, limerence makes us down-grade the differences between us and our beloved (because we are so keen on achieving union with them). It makes us overlook any potential conflicts and interpret anything – however contrary to everyday experience – as positive for the relation-ship. This is probably why Ryan misread the signs and felt so let down. After his girlfriend left him, he spiralled into depression: 'I couldn't concen-trate. I skipped lectures and failed to hand in a crucial essay on time.' If you, too, are suffering from the fallout from limerence, see Chapter Seven for more advice.

If limerence generally lasts for at least six months at the bottom end of the scale, what is the top end? In my experience, limerence normally lasts somewhere between eighteen months and three years. Fortunately, the 'blindness' lessens towards the second half of this period and reality intrudes. Slowly but surely, a couple can assess whether there is a long-term future for their relationship. It is at this point that couples begin to develop what I call 'loving attachment'. The good news is that loving attachment, unlike limerence, can last for a lifetime. (For more information on how to nurture and protect loving attachment, see another book in this series: *Build a Life-long Love Affair*.)

When I explain the concept of limerence, some of my clients are rather disappointed. Reciprocated limerence is wonderful, one of life's joys. Why can't it last for ever? First, it would not be practical to be forever sitting around mooning over our beloved. We'd never get round to raising any children and mankind would probably still be living in mud huts. Second, under the influence of limerence, we make many bad relationship choices. We convince ourselves that wholly impractical people will make perfect partners, or throw ourselves into hopeless and painful affairs. Yet without a burst of limerence, I doubt that two people would ever launch themselves into the adventure of a shared life. How else would anyone be crazy enough to trust a complete stranger with their future?

So if you are currently under the influence of limerence, surrender to the experience and enjoy every moment. The fact that it will not last for ever should make every moment of bliss that little bit sweeter.

The Eighteen Months Test

If three months is the moment where casual going out becomes a full-blown relationship, eighteen months is when that relationship turns into a committed partnership. The crazy peak of limerence, where you cannot eat, work or think straight, has passed but there is enough bliss left to smooth over the tensions of moving in together. Scientific evidence backs up my theory that this is the crucial window of opportunity. Long-term tracking by the University of Texas has found that an eighteen-months to three-year courtship is the optimum period for a happy marriage. Indeed, social biologists discovered that dopamine, phenylethylamine and oxytocin, the three hormones responsible for love and bonding, are at their height for eighteen months to three years too.

The final piece of evidence comes from the market researcher, John T. Molloy, who interviewed 2,500 couples leaving American marriage bureaux (*Why Men Marry Some Women and Not Others*, Warner Books, 2004). He also identifies eighteen months as the time courting couples are most likely to become engaged. In his opinion, by twenty-two months the chance of a proposal begins to dip slightly. Then, over the next year and a half, the odds diminish gradually. After three and a half years together, however, the odds of a couple making a lasting commitment begins to plummet.

So answer the following questions about your relationship:

1. If someone attractive shows an interest in you, would you tell him or her that you're already seeing someone?
2. Would your boyfriend or girlfriend do the same?

3. Is your lover the person to whom you tell the ins and outs of your day?

4. Do you enjoy just hanging out together without some structured activity – like going to a movie or dining out?

5. Could you discuss and book next year's summer holiday or discuss plans for Christmas?

6. Does the way that your lover talks about the relationship match with his or her actual behaviour?

7. Do you both want the same things out of life?

8. If you had an emergency – for instance, if your house was broken into – would your lover be the first person you would phone for emotional and practical support?

9. If you had good news, would your lover be the first person you would call?

10. Do you generally put each other's interests first?

11. Can you confide your inner secrets, fears and dreams?

12. Would your lover protect you against a personal attack from his or her family?

13. Can you cooperate and organise a major event together – like a touring holiday or a big party?

14. Would you describe your beloved as a good person?

There is no pass or fail score on this test, but you should hope to be able to answer 'yes' to at least the first seven questions.

From here onwards, each question reveals progressively important qualities about your relationship. When I discuss this test with clients, they expect support through adversity to be the key test. However, whether or not our beloved can truly share in our success is more important; often our partner fears that it will take us away from them. I've put cooperating and organising even further down the list because successful relationships are all about teamwork, so this is another make-or-break issue.

Moving on to question fourteen, I would be concerned if you answered 'yes' but added a rider. For example: 'as long as she has not had too much to drink' or 'as long as he controls his jealousy'. How likely is this to happen? What is the opinion of people who really care about you?

There are two more questions in the eighteen months test:

15. How old is your beloved?
16. How many of their ambitions have they achieved?

If you want to get married, or to make a commitment for life, these two final questions are the most important. Let me explain why. The average age of a first marriage in the United Kingdom is thirty for men and twenty-eight for women. Our thirties are the prime period for settling down because by forty-five, only 6 per cent of women and 9 per cent of men have never married. Age is also a crucial issue for women who want to settle down and have a family. However, contrary to popular wisdom, men have a biological clock too – which begins to tick at around forty-two. Men are not so worried about being able to father a child as whether they will still have enough energy to be an active father.

Moving on to ambition, rightly or wrongly, most men still expect to be the principal bread-winner and will not consider settling down and starting a family until they are established in their careers or have achieved their ambitions. Take Simon, a thirty-six-year-old photographer who, finally, is looking for a partner: 'Previously, I wanted the freedom to do what I wanted, when I wanted.' He had been in a steady relationship between the ages of nineteen and twenty-one but found the love of his girlfriend restrictive: 'It was all going round the shops on Saturdays and roast dinners with her parents on Sundays. I wanted to see jungles, volcanoes and sail south of the equator.' Men who have been to university – and therefore who take longer to get established on the career ladder – get married later. Their prime window is thirty to thirty-six (towards the top end of this range, if they take a second degree or undertake further training). In contrast, men who are not university graduates marry between twenty-eight and thirty-three.

Although a man or a woman might be determined to make their mark on the world, and worry that the demands of a clinging partner might hold them back, they have not taken a vow of celibacy. Charlie, thirty-two, has a successful career in the City which involves a lot of business trips – as he says: 'I have to travel light'. However, that did not stop him falling in love: 'It was wonderful and horrible. I felt ill. I couldn't think of anything beyond her, she bled into everything else I did and it was all wonderful. I felt magnetic.' Unfortunately, she wanted a family and they eventually split. As Charlie summed it up: 'Right girl but the wrong time.'

It is easy to paint men like Charlie as 'lying bastards' but he insists that he was up-front about not wanting a serious relationship: 'Time after time, I thought everything was on the table but we'd still end up in bars with her crying, "but I love you".'

It is not just men who want a little 'uncomplicated' affection. I've had complaints from older divorced men who miss the warmth and companionship of a relationship but cannot find a woman interested in a committed relationship. Take Greg, forty-eight, who has been on the singles scene for three years: 'I'm amazed by all these predatory women in their fifties. Don't get me wrong, they're beautiful and they keep their bodies in amazing shape, but they have their lives sorted: nice flat and car, good circle of friends, and they don't want it complicated by a full-time man. There was one woman, the sex was incredible, but the closer we got the more she kept slipping away, until suddenly she was gone.'

Moving in Together

You have successfully negotiated 'seeing each other' into boyfriend and girlfriend, and you can broach the 'commitment' word without either one of you disappearing – so moving in together should be relatively straightforward – especially as you have spent most weekends, and often a week night too, round each other's flats. So what could possibly go wrong?

The first trend is that we are waiting longer to start a serious relationship. Although it is useful to know yourself before settling down, it does make it harder to compromise. 'I was looking forward to coming home to someone, rather than to an empty flat,' says Sarah, a thirty-two-year-old lawyer. 'I'd been in student halls and done flat shares after I graduated, so I was used to getting on with other people. Yet I can't believe how annoyed I get when Anthony uses the same chopping board for meat and vegetables. OK, he thinks I'm a hygiene freak, but once he bought some wet fish home and the whole kitchen stank as he moved the drippy bag from one work surface to another!'

When Sarah and Anthony had been dating, they had seldom cooked in each other's kitchens. 'When I did use her utensils, I would respect her rules and her ideas of the best place to keep them – but I don't want to spend the rest of my life seeing salmonella lurking in every corner,' explains Anthony. They had spent so long living alone, and not having to consider other people, that they found it harder to see any view beyond their own.

Another problem is that living together means different things to different people. For Tom, in his early thirties, it was a practical matter: 'Nicole's lease was up, so I offered to clear some drawers and space in the wardrobe. I thought she'd be pleased but, for some reason, she sulked for the rest of the weekend.' For Nicole, a twenty-nine-year-old office space planner, living together was a sign of commitment: 'I felt our relationship had reached that stage and for it continue to grow we should live together. I wanted a proper invitation and a declaration about how much he loved me – rather than a couple of empty drawers.' When I pressed her further, she admitted certain expectations: 'OK, I saw us a step closer to settling down and having children together.' Like many people today, Nicole saw moving in as a commitment almost on a par with walking down the aisle. However, while marriage has clear obligations, backed by law, living together is open to many different interpretations.

With most people I counsel, the transition from part-time to full-time couple would have been easier if they had been aware of the pitfalls. So what should you expect? First, the rules for staying round at your partner's house are very different from those when you are living together.

'Jodie likes the television on during the night, or her iPod on shuffle, because it covers the noise outside,' explains Carl, thirty-three, who had just moved into her flat, 'but it stops me dropping into a really deep sleep and I've reached the point where I think I'm going to explode.'

'But you never complained before – well, not much,' countered Jodie.

'If I had a bad night, I could go home and catch up – and, anyway, we'd mainly sleep together at the weekend when I didn't have to get up early,' he answered.

Previously, Carl had been a guest in Jodie's flat but since he was now paying half the bills, he had dug in his heels.

When dating, time spent together is nearly always quality time. Nicole expected the same level of attention when she started cohabiting. 'I am completely exhausted when I get home,' says Tom. 'I have to sit down with a glass of wine and unwind before I can cope with any kind of human interaction.' Nicole had been looking forward to seeing him and would feel neglected and unloved. This re-entry point from working into couple time is crucial, and for Tom and Nicole it would set up either a good or a bad evening together. In coun-selling, we found a compromise where they would quickly share the headlines from their day, then Tom would have his quiet time and the couple would properly catch up over supper.

Another complication was that Tom belonged to the first generation of men raised by mothers who expected the same things from both their sons and daughters. 'I was pleased that Tom was prepared to use the vacuum cleaner and do things that my father would never even have considered,' says Nicole, 'but I never thought he'd have such strong ideas about interior design. We had a horrible row in the DIY superstore about what colour to paint the chimney breast – while my father would not have cared if Mum wanted the whole house vermilion.' In previous generations, jobs were split down gender lines; now it is more down to taste and ability – which takes more negotiation.

Jealousy about past relationships can also become acute after a couple move in together. There is a big difference between knowing about his ex and finding a box of photographs recording all their golden moments together in your home.

'It was not just photographs but cinema stubs and other mementoes,' says Candida, a twenty-seven-year-old marketing executive. 'I know I shouldn't have looked but I couldn't stop myself. There was a picture of the two of them together in Paris; he'd taken me there for a wonderful weekend but never told me he'd been there with her too.'

Candida did not want to appear paranoid, so had said nothing. Should she bring it up? Should he be hanging on to his past? In counselling, we began to get to the bottom of the issue: 'I want him to say that he loves me more than her,' Candida admitted. 'But he lives with you not her,' I replied, and out came all her worries about cohabitation which had been hidden behind her jealousy.

Even the happiest couples have disagreements when they start to live together – it is part of the natural evolution of a relationship. So what is the secret to minimising them? First, accept that we are territorial animals. It helps to move into a neutral space. If this is not possible, allow your partner to make his or her mark on your place or, if you are moving into his or her space, agree on a makeover beforehand. Next, give each other time to adjust and accept that rows are a vital part of forging a life together. It is better to get things out in the open than to bite your tongue and store up problems for the future.

When it comes to the sticking points, remember there are two options: changing your partner or changing yourself. Although there should be a bit of both, ultimately it is easier to change your own attitude. Let go of the small stuff – like where to keep the bin bags – so that the battles are over truly non-negotiable issues. Finally, remind yourself of all the benefits: just chilling on the sofa together, doing fun things on the spur of the moment and being at the centre of someone else's life.

TOP FIVE FLASH POINTS FOR MOVING IN TOGETHER

1. **Chores.** You expect more help when someone lives with you 24/7 and different standards of cleanliness and tidiness come to the fore.

2. **Stuff.** With two sets of crockery, beds and pictures, what do you keep and what goes? Some items might have sentimental value, but do you really want something bought by a previous partner?

3. **Social life.** Previously, what you did during the week was a private matter, but now it has an impact on your partner too. How much couple time and how much individual time is right for you?

4. **Different tastes.** You were aware of your partner's hobbies or interests before, but knowing just how long someone spends on the computer or talking to their mother on the phone can turn them from accepted into contentious issues.

5. **Sex.** With maximum opportunity for lovemaking comes maximum opportunity for being turned down; a new pattern for when to be sexual together needs to emerge.

Life Milestones

There are three times when couples are particularly likely to drift apart – not because there is something fundamentally wrong with their relationship but because life milestones are putting them under increased pressure.

The baby blues

Although bringing up the next generation is possibly the most fulfilling and life-affirming thing anyone can do, babies do seem to have a mission to destroy everything from your clothes and furniture to your nerves, sex life and even your marriage.

Breakthrough tip: We have a very clear idea of what it means to be a mother or a father – partly from watching movies and reading books but mainly from our own experiences of being a child. Unfortunately, every family is different and instead of talking about what our own mum and dad did, we assume our partner will have the same take on dividing up the jobs.

Matt and Sandra, in their mid-thirties, came to counselling over rows about Matt not pulling his weight. 'But I play with the children when I get home and take our son to the park and read stories,' Matt complained. 'You get the fun bits and leave me with all the dirty business,' Sandra countered.

Instead of letting them getting into another round of 'who has it toughest', I asked Matt to talk about his own father and mother: 'I suppose he did get the best bits, he was always making puppet theatres and giving us treats. Mum was the one that did all the disciplining.'

'What impact did that have on your relationship with your mother? I asked.

'I suppose it wasn't really fair on her and we've only got closer since I've had children myself.'

With their expectations on the table, rather than hidden away, Matt and Sandra were ready to sort out the parenting that suited them rather than repeating their own parents' choices.

Mid-life readjustment

Although we know that we are not immortal, the full implications only hit us when someone close dies or we reach the midpoint in our life. This is normally a time of reflection: looking back over the first half of our life and making plans for the second. If someone has been focused on earning money and work, there is normally a desire to do something more meaningful or achieve some, as yet unfulfilled, ambition. If someone has been more family focused, they will want to make their mark on the outside world.

Many experts dub this the 'mid-life crisis', but I don't see it as a crisis, more a challenge and, in some cases, a relief, because the old life-style no longer works for us. However, if any mild twinges of dread, disappointment and rest-lessness – the early warning signs of a need for change – are ignored, they can build into panic, fear and an overwhelming sense of loss. If this sounds familiar and you feel unable to discuss your feelings with your partner, your partner has belittled or dismissed what you're going through, or you feel trapped by the need to earn money or by the family's expectations, there is a real danger of a mid-life adjustment turning into a relationship crisis.

'I caught my reflection getting out of the bath and I didn't recognise this lumpy guy with a paunch. I used to be really sporty,' says Robert, forty-two. 'I used to really enjoy life but I'd started having a really short temper. I needed space, the children got on my nerves, work was not giving me any satisfaction. Where was my life going?' Everything came to a head after reorganisation at work and Robert had felt sidelined by the new team. 'I found out about a strategy meeting but I wasn't invited. I felt invisible to my boss, my wife and my kids. Just someone who paid the bills.' These sorts of feelings explain why both men and women are particularly vulnerable to affairs at this life milestone: attention from someone attractive (and possibly younger) boosts self-esteem and seems to provide some direction.

Breakthrough tip: Write a letter to yourself at eighteen. What advice would you give? What knowledge does your younger self need? What surprises has the first half of your life thrown at you? Read back the letter and look at how the advice to the eighteen-year-old might be applicable today.

Instead of focusing on what you are losing, start thinking about what you want. What are you not doing? Once you can voice your desires – however impossible they might sound – there is a way out of depression or feeling trapped in a dead-end. Finally, ask yourself: How could my partner help on this new journey and how could I bring him or her on side?

Empty nest

Sometimes couples are so good at being parents that they lose each other in the bustle of family life. This is why the most common problem brought to university student welfare counsellors is 'my parents have just split up'. In most cases, this is a complete surprise because their mother and father seemed to get on so well. Often a mid-life adjustment and empty nest coincide to bring one of the most dangerous times for a relationship. If the thought of your children leaving home fills you with dread or loneliness, it is important to act rather than hope things will get better.

Breakthrough tip: Ask for what you want, rather than complain about what you don't. The first invites a discussion, the second will put your partner's back up. It also helps to be specific. Instead of asking 'Why don't we go travelling?', suggest learning to scuba dive and exploring the Great Barrier Reef together. Not everything that you want or your partner wants will appeal to both of you. However, keep an open mind and at least try out his or her ideas. With a bit of experimenting, you will find a new path or a new project together. So don't be afraid to think big.

Summing Up

Three months is a good time to stop and assess the potential of your relationship. However, make certain that you listen attentively so that you hear what is said rather than what you want to hear. The ecstasy of limerence can blind people to the true character of their beloved and the relationship. Only when limerence has subsided – probably at around eighteen months – can you begin to judge whether this is lasting love or not. Remember, change is inevitable and, as relationships grow, the upheaval can make you question your love.

IN A NUTSHELL:

- However long the two of you have been together, negotiating is one of the key ingredients for surviving change.
- Don't hold back about what is important to you. Compromising too soon, before you have really laid out your cases and your needs, will leave you feeling resentful and store up problems for the future.
- Really listen to your partner's ideas, ask questions and find out more about his or her hopes and fears. Only when you truly understand each other's viewpoints can you begin to discuss the future.

STEP 6

DECISION TIME

Most people who can't make up their mind are trying to weigh up the pros and cons about their relationship. But how can you balance the present issues and an uncertain future? Should 'but I love him or her' trump infuriating or destructive behaviour? No wonder people find themselves going round in circles.

Instead of putting your relationship on trial like a lawyer or a judge, my advice is to approach it like a doctor and make a diagnosis. So the sixth main question in my programme is:

Are you asking the right questions?

In this chapter, I ask questions that allow you to look deeper than everyday surface issues and to discover what's really happening. If you come back with reassuringly positive answers, your relationship has a clean bill and you can look forward to a healthy future together.

Decision-making and the New Relationship

Question one: How good were the good times? Sometimes when people look back at the beginning of the relationship, they discover that it was not as brilliant as they first thought. 'It seemed so good on paper – great restaurant, handsome guy, good job – but now I wonder how much my imagination and my hopes filled in the gaps,' said Alannah, thirty-two, when she looked back at her first dates with David, thirty-six. 'Did my fantasies also inflate OK sex into great sex?' It is important to take the rose-coloured glasses off because although you can fix what is broken, you can't fix what was never right.

Question two: Are you listening to what your partner says but ignoring what he or she actually does? This was the clincher for Alannah. 'He says all the right things. He loves me, he's really keen on me. He can see a future for us,' she explained, 'but he seldom calls when he says he will. He gets really vague when I want to plan something, even if it's only a couple of months ahead.'

Conversely, for Miranda, twenty-nine, this question allowed her to drop her barriers and let her new boyfriend in. 'He had always been reticent with his feelings, so I thought he didn't really care, until I was ill and he arrived at my home with a saucepan of home-made soup.'

Question three: Is your partner genuinely interested in what you're doing? 'I would listen to all the intricacies of his latest business deals and even work up an interest in his kite boarding,' explains Emily, thirty-six, 'but he could not even remember my best friend's name.' On her next date, she monitored how much time he talked about himself and his reaction when the conversation turned to her. 'What really shocked me was how his eyes seemed to glaze over, or he'd be looking for the waiter for another drink if I talked about something that interested me.' It also became clear that his lifestyle – weekends away kite boarding – excluded her. Emily, rightly, concluded that he was not into her enough to make this a viable long-term relationship.

Question four: How does he or she make you feel about yourself? Although a supportive and caring partner can boost your confidence and feeling of self-worth, it is not their job to make you feel good about yourself. So this question is about how your boyfriend or girlfriend makes you feel above and beyond your usual feelings about yourself. Does being with him improve your self-respect or, if you contradict her, does she make you feel crazy or stupid? Can you relax and be yourself or do you always feel on trial?

Julia, forty-eight, ran her own successful small business but left school at sixteen. Her boyfriend, Mark, forty-nine, had been to a leading university. 'If something intellectual comes up – some so-called famous writer or composer – he has this horrible habit of explaining who he is and what he's done. It not only drives me up the wall, but also makes me feel stupid too.' It was especially hurtful when he did it in front of friends.

Although a negative response to this question was a black mark against their relationship, before you make a definitive decision about yours, look at the next question.

Question five: Is anything off the table? By this I mean: can you talk about anything and everything?

When I looked at this question with Julia, she decided that she would talk to Mark about his intellectual name-dropping. She reported back the next week: 'I told him how belittled I felt and got a surprise. He does it to include me in the conversation.' They went on to have a long and fruitful discussion and agreed that, in the future, Julia would ask if she wanted an explanation. The more subjects that can be on the table, the healthier the relationship will be. Indeed, Julia and Mark went on to get married. Conversely, when I put this question to Rebecca there was something important that her boyfriend refused to discuss: 'I knew he wanted to go back to Australia, but he would just evade the topic.' Ultimately, he did return – alone.

Question six: Do both of you look forward to touching each other? The previous questions have been aimed at understanding whether your partner is into you enough for your relationship to have a future. This one, and the next, focuses on whether you are into him or her enough. 'My boyfriend is really nice. He's understanding, he treats me well and he's a good listener too,' said Alison, twenty-eight. Her boyfriend had passed all the previous questions but she got stuck on this one. 'I have to admit there's no real spark.' She stopped for a moment and looked down. 'If I'm honest, it's fine when there're other people around, but if we're alone for too long he can really get on my nerves.' It turned out that Alison liked his family – especially his mother and sister – more than him. Although relationships are not just about sex, it is important to have good physical chemistry. Alison did end the relationship and even though he seemed a good prospect for a long-term relationship, she has not regretted her decision.

Question seven: Have you been down this road before? Look back at your last few boyfriends; do the relationships all follow a similar pattern? Do you fall for men who cannot commit? Do you always date nice boys but lust after bad ones? Do you always date clinging women or, when things get serious, do you melt away? When Jodie, forty-three, stripped away the outward differences between her previous boyfriends and instead concentrated on how they all made her feel, she had a revelation: 'I would go out with musicians, actors, models. They were all really interesting, talented and had troubled pasts – or liked to drink too much. I was always trying to motivate them or throwing away old pizza boxes from their living rooms.' It became clear that she fell for their potential rather than the reality. So I asked about her current boy-friend. Jodie laughed because he was cut from the same cloth, and history had just told her that this relationship would go the same way.

When Jeremy, the forty-seven-year-old actor, answered this question, he realised that he had started seeing yet another woman who had only recently separated from her husband – his sixth in a row. 'Her relationship ended a year ago,' he said, trying to sound hopeful. However, there is often a difference between the 'official' end and the 'actual' end. All those meetings hoping to change his or her mind, that time when they had sex for old times' sake, they all count. Jeremy knew all about this from his own divorce: 'We had lots of attempts at reconciliation and I do wonder if my girlfriend is truly over her ex.' He thought for a moment. 'Yes, it does seem that I'm rescuing her from her past rather than starting the sort of committed relationship that I'm seeking.'

Weighing up the evidence

These seven questions should help cut through the fog that can easily obscure your view of the future. Hopefully, your new boyfriend or girl-friend has passed with flying colours and you will feel more confident about letting down your guard and taking a risk. If he or she failed, talk about how you are feeling. Maybe you will get a pleasant surprise and your partner will fight for you; maybe he or she will agree that the relationship has no future. Whichever way, you will have clarity.

When I did this quiz with Maxine – who was worried about a possible Christmas proposal – her boyfriend passed with flying colours. As she wanted a family, I threw in an extra question: 'How would you feel if you had a child just like your partner?' Maxine had no trouble with this one either: 'I'd be delighted.' However, something was still holding her back. When I delved deeper, I discovered that she had met Jamie, thirty-four, just seven weeks after her husband left her. She had been invited by a friend on a holiday abroad to recover, and Jamie had been another house guest. Three years later, Maxine was divorced and considered herself over her ex but, on several occasions, presented a very different picture. 'I was really pleased to discover that the woman that my ex left me for ended up cheating on him,' she said gleefully. If Maxine had been truly over him, she would not have cared one way or the other.

In general, it takes two years to recover fully from marital breakdown. It seemed Maxine had found the right man but still she needed to work on understanding what went wrong in her marriage and on learning the lessons before she would be ready to marry Jamie.

If you are still undecided about whether to commit or not, I have one further thought: nobody is ready for marriage or living together. Marriage makes you ready for marriage. By this I mean the very act of committing makes you more committed. Why should this be? A raft of experiments have given people something for nothing – like a coffee mug – and then negotiated a price to buy it back. The price that someone places on the mug shoots up the moment they possess it. In fact, this figure is normally twice as high as another random person, off the street, would pay for the mug.

ACTING 'AS IF'

This is the best piece of advice that I have ever received. But first, let me give you a bit of background. I once interviewed a woman whose daughter was found face down in a neighbour's pond. The child was resuscitated but did not have a heartbeat for forty minutes and was left severely handicapped. Her mother blamed herself as she had left her daughter in the care of a nanny. It is hard to think of anything worse and I asked this woman how she kept going. 'Of course, there are times when I want to lock myself in a small dark room and scream and scream. Except my daughter needs me and I have another able-bodied child, a husband and a business. People are counting on me. When I think I can't go on, I remember this wonderful woman who shared her secret with me. "Act as if you can cope. At first it will be just that – an act. But after a while, you'll find yourself acting less and being more. Suddenly, one day, you will find that it is no longer an act and you can actually cope."'

So this exercise is simple. Next time you find yourself facing an obstacle ask yourself: How would I behave if I was committed to this relationship? Once the picture is firmly in your head, imagine the first step and act as if you believed in your relationship. Pretty soon, you too will stop acting and be committed.

Decision-making and the Established Relationship

Question one: Does your partner accept that there is a problem? When Martha thought about this question, she knew that her relationship was over. 'He just bats my concerns away: "I'm perfectly happy" or "Life isn't a bed of roses" or "You knew what I was like when we married".' Conversely, even if your partner seems to have little motivation for changing things but agrees that your relationship could be better, there is still hope. Your partner is possibly resistant because he or she is frightened rather than has a closed mind.

Question two: Do you focus more on what your partner does *not* do and overlook what he or she does do? It is human nature to be preoccupied with what we need and forget about what we already have. But if you step into your partner's shoes for a moment, the small and large acts of service – such as being chief breadwinner or being responsible for the lion's share of running the house – need to be acknowledged before he or she can offer anything more.

Valerie desperately needed her husband to open up to her – especially since their eldest daughter married and their youngest needed her less: 'Recently, my husband started talking about how tired he felt after the long commute home and, instead of leaping in with how tired I was, I asked about the daily journey, how he felt about work, and he explained how little he enjoyed his work but felt he had no choice because it paid the bills. Instead of pitching in with how much I earned, I thought about all those years, all those train journeys and the sacrifices he'd made to make us all secure. We talked some more and I realised that he had confided in me.' Valerie's husband had shown his love in practical ways. Valerie, herself, showed hers through words and talking about intimate matters. However, just because your partner does not express his or her love in the same way as you do, it does not make it any less valid.

Question three: Does your partner show a concrete interest in your projects or offer some practical support? Love is not just saying 'I love you' but is holding the welfare of your beloved close to your heart and being prepared to deliver on it.

When Patricia decided to train as an aerobics instructor, she had to go away for training weekends. 'My husband works at the weekend and even though I gave him plenty of notice, he was not prepared to take time off to look after the kids because his free time was "precious", so I had to ask my mum. When I came back, he asked how it went but didn't show any real interest or ask further questions.' Although this alone was not enough for Patricia to leave, it was a major black mark against her husband and internally she withdrew from him. Ultimately, the couple separated five years later.

Question four: Could you give more even if there was no immediate hope of being paid back? Frequently, I counsel couples where both partners are angry and exhausted. Each feels that he or she has given a lot; each is waiting for the other to make the first move. In effect, they are in deadlock. However, if you are prepared to do something nice – and it doesn't have to be much – like smile, concede some bone of contention with good grace, help your partner with something or give a compliment, there is life still left in your relationship. This will not only break the deadlock and improve the atmosphere in the house but also, doing something nice will make you feel better too. Over time, and it will probably take a few weeks, your partner will begin to respond more positively too and you will be getting on well enough to start working on improving your relationship.

What about the opposite? I once counselled a couple who could think of nothing kind to do for each other. Even flicking on the kettle before leaving for work in the morning, so that the other came down to hot water for a cup of tea, was too much trouble. It was too late. This relationship was already dead and the next week they gave up counselling.

Question five: Is your partner interested in getting close only so that he or she can be angry or critical? When you let down your guard and become vulnerable, how does your partner respond? Is an apology accepted with good grace or do you open the floodgate for a snub ('I should think so too') or, worse still, more criticism ('This wouldn't happen if you thought things through')? When you talk over a problem, do you get sympathy and advice or simply put-downs? Do any attempts to talk through your problems become an excuse for recriminations? Although everybody's partner says hurtful things from time to time – mainly out of thoughtlessness rather than anything more sinister – this anger seems almost constant. If you have answered yes to this question, your relationship is in a very dangerous place. Although the opposite of love is not hatred – as many people think – but indifference, it is very hard to come back from here.

Question six: Do you ever have fun together? There might be only one or two oases of calm in your relationship, but these can be the launching pad for improving your communication and can show that you can cooperate enough to work on your sex life too. Howard and Natalie, whom we met in Chapter Two, took a bath together most days and enjoyed family days out. We expanded on this and Natalie went to watch Howard play football (she had not done that since they first dated) and volunteered to help at the supporters' coffee stand. She made friends with other soccer wives and they started socialising together. Meanwhile, Howard helped Natalie's art club make stands for their latest exhibition and decided to join too. Even small amounts of fun together can be the starting point for something very positive.

Question seven: Have you learned something from reading this book which makes it either impossible to leave or impossible to stay? As you work through this book, certain exercises, case histories or pieces of advice will start you thinking. Let these thoughts brew for a couple of days. They have caught your imagination for a reason. How could you apply them to your situation?

Weighing up the evidence

Hopefully, these seven questions will have helped you find clarity. With long-standing relationships, the stakes are higher. There is more invested in the relationship and, if you have children together, you are bonded – even if only as co-parents – for life. So take your time and discuss your findings with your partner.

If you are still undecided, I would advise getting professional help from a qualified couple counsellor. If your partner is non-committal, or even hostile, still make an appointment. Many partners will come to the first session to discover what counselling involves. If he or she still refuses, go into counselling yourself and maybe your partner will join in later.

CHANGING YOUR NEGATIVE MINDSET

Sometimes people are still stuck because a little voice in their head is pulling them down or making them depressed:

1. **Recognise the thoughts.** Often they happen so quickly and are so well rehearsed that they pass unnoticed and unchallenged. So write them all down, as if you are taking dictation.

2. **Dispute automatic thoughts.** In many cases, personal interpretations of events are accepted as facts, rather than just opinions.

3. **Look for exaggerations.** Have you built a cast-iron case out of a few bad experiences?

4. **Find alternative interpretations.** In particular, ones that are less personal, less permanent and less pervasive.

5. **What conclusions might an optimist draw?** Imagine for a moment that you are an optimist and look at the same information again. How does this change your opinion?

Summing Up

Instead of weighing up the pros and cons of staying together, make a diagnosis about the overall health of your relationship. If you are still unsure, give your partner the benefit of the doubt and throw yourself into working on your relationship (but review in three months). It is better to do something positive than to do nothing or simply snipe from the sidelines.

IN A NUTSHELL:

- Don't wait for your partner to pull you out of limbo by making up his or her mind; take responsibility for your happiness.
- Look at whether your relationship is healthy enough to be saved.
- Don't be afraid to get help from professionals, friends or family.

STEP 7

TURNING YOUR DECISION INTO A REALITY

By this point in the journey, you should have decided if your partner is right for you or not. However, making a decision and acting on it are two different things. So the last question is:

How can I move forward?

You might have made up your mind but that's only half the equation. What about your partner? How does he or she feel?

There are three possible outcomes. Your partner will agree with your decision (so you can move in together/get married, recommit to your relationship or separate amicably), or be ambivalent (and need convincing) or, finally, he or she could disagree vehemently. Each of these scenarios can throw up problems which knock you off your chosen course. In this chapter, I will help you deal with the fallout from coming out of limbo.

Turn Your New Relationship into a Committed Partnership

There are many couples who take the eighteen months test and find that they are not ready to make a long-term commitment. My message is 'don't panic'. There is still time to overcome the obstacles and turn the answers from negative to positive.

It is easier for a man in love. He can cut through the confusion with a proposal. It's romantic and gets all the issues on the table. A woman in love has to be more tactical and engineer a conversation about the future. Although an ultimatum to 'marry me, move in with me, or else I'll move on' might seem straightforward and honest, nobody responds well to threats. Instead, make it clear that you are the 'marrying kind' or 'need a proper commitment' and discover where both of you stand. It will be difficult but, by the eighteen months point, your relationship will be robust enough to cope with a bit of conflict.

Hopefully, the conversation will go smoothly, but if there are sticking points, or he says something hurtful, be careful not to overreact. This is important for two reasons. First, you do not want your future together to become such a toxic subject that it is hard to bring up again. Second, you may be so fearful of rejection that you have projected outright defeat on to a position of nuance. So instead of rowing, sulking or storming off, return to the conversation the next day or when your beloved is in a good mood. The aim is to seek clarification. 'I'm not ready' can mean both 'no' and something more ambivalent.

Take Charlie, from Chapter Five, and his 'right girl, wrong time': 'I wanted children but I needed two more years.' Unfortunately, he had not had this conversation with his girlfriend and she left without knowing the full picture. Another common phrase that can mean different things to different people is 'some day'. This can be a nice way of saying 'never' or it could mean a specific date.

Sometimes attempts to clarify a beloved's position are met with more blocking. If this is the case, try an old trick that I learned as a journalist dealing with the police – who are notorious for keeping facts to themselves. It's called fishing.

When someone claims 'I don't know', you guess a possible answer, for example: 'twelve to eighteen months'. Normally the other person will either agree or correct you. If you get a second 'I don't know', try fishing once more. For example: 'longer or less' can sometimes trigger a ballpark prediction. However, if your partner genuinely doesn't know, let the subject drop or you risk a pointless row.

The other useful response to 'I'm not ready' is so simple that many people overlook it. Try asking: Why? There could be a perfectly under-standable reason: 'I'm worried about my student debts' or 'I'm saving for a deposit'. However, if you are still upset by his or her response, you need to make the following points:

- **Reassurance.** 'I love you but I'm disappointed because I was hoping to spend the rest of my life with you.'
- **Explanation.** 'I'm hurt because I thought the relationship was going somewhere.'
- **Reassertion.** 'Children/marriage is important to my happiness.'

Generally, a tactical retreat is better than contin-uing to repeat the same point. At eighteen months, there is still enough time and sometimes when one partner stops pushing that is the moment when the other partner changes his or her mind.

Sometimes when the cards go on the table at eighteen months, a couple will discover very different agendas. Here is an example from my counselling casebook: 'I really enjoy going out, doing stuff with Ellis. The sex is great and she might even be the "one",' says Martin who is thirty-four, 'except she already has her family and, to be honest, much as I like her kids, I wouldn't want to miss out.' 'But what about Ellis, doesn't she have expectations?' I asked. Martin looked down at his shoes and mumbled. It was obvious that Martin and Ellis had avoided this conversation. Martin wanted the benefits of a relationship 'for now' and although Ellis seemed to want a commitment, she was afraid to force the issue. Sadly, the couple separated.

Generally, if there is no commitment by two years together, and commitment is important to you, I would suggest becoming less available or stopping seeing your partner altogether. (See the exercise on the next page.) In some cases, a retreat will change your partner's mind but be aware that he or she might also disappear.

What if you want to commit to your new relationship but your partner is truly not interested? This is hard, especially when you are head over heels in love. However, it is not impossible, as the following exercise shows.

COMING DOWN OFF THE LIMERENCE HIGH

It is impossible to escape limerence until one of the following conditions have been met:

a) **Consummation:** The bliss of reciprocation is gradually either blended into a lasting love or replaced by less positive feelings.

b) **Starvation:** Even under the spell of limerence it becomes harder and harder to interpret the actions of someone not interested into positive signs of hope. It is finally accepted that the object of limerence does not return the feelings.

c) **Transformation:** Attentions are transferred to a new person. (This normally overlaps with Starvation, because someone at the height of limerence is unable even to consider an alternative partner.)

So if you find yourself trapped in limerence with someone who doesn't return your feelings, here are some tips on achieving Starvation:

- Try not to indulge yourself with fantasies of how it could all come right in the end. Although this might provide a few moments of pleasure, it will only increase your pain.

- If you find yourself weakening, use a distraction technique – such as doing some exercise or phoning a friend.

- Don't torture yourself. Put all the photographs and keepsakes in the loft. Find different ways to work that do not involve going past the favourite restaurant that the two of you shared together. Don't put on his favourite music or read books by her favourite author.

- Disconnect your thoughts. When you find your-self thinking: 'I wonder if he would have liked this film?' or 'What would she have looked like in that dress?' put up a mental STOP sign and think of something mundane – like what to buy at the supermarket.

- Cut the links. If you have mutual friends, stop seeing them for a while. If you are honest, you probably decided to go out with them in the hope of either hearing about your beloved or getting them to pass on informa-tion about you.

- Forget closure. It is tempting to think 'If only I could understand why she is not interested' or

'If only I got my own back on her' that you would feel better. However, these thoughts just preserve the links.

- Remember, Starvation needs time. Six months on a strict regime should cure most cases. If you are still stuck, ask yourself: 'What is the benefit in staying where I am?' Common reasons for not moving on include: punishing yourself, punishing your beloved (when he or she hears how miserable I am then he or she will be sorry), fear of making a new relationship.

How to Recommit to Your Long-term Relationship

Deciding to give your partner another chance is only the beginning of the journey; you have to cut through years of misunderstandings, upset and neglect. To kick-start this process, here are six ways to revitalise your relationship:

1. **Look at each other more.** Couples in love spend 75 per cent of their time looking at each other when they are talking, rather than the usual 30 per cent to 60 per cent.

2. **Go that extra mile.** Unfortunately, we take the everyday gestures – such as cooking or filling up the car with petrol – for granted. However, we notice the special things and being extra kind will encourage him or her to reciprocate.

3. **Stop editing your day.** We imagine that our partner is not interested in the minutiae of our lives but the less we hear, the less we care. So save up colourful incidents from your day to share in the evening.

4. **Enjoy casual body contact.** Cuddling on the sofa, stroking and kissing should be enjoyed in their own right, rather than just as a prelude to intercourse.

5. **Laugh together.** Private jokes and teasing can really feed a relationship. Alternatively, go to a comedy club or see a funny film together.

6. **Pretend that you don't know each other.** Psychologists at the universities of British Columbia and Virginia discovered that we treat strangers better than our partners – as we hope that this will make them like us. So the researchers asked couples to interact as though they had never met before and found that their well-being rose significantly. So why not meet your partner in a bar or some other public space, pretend to be strangers and chat

each other up? You will probably learn something new about each other and have a good laugh too.

If you are keen to try again at your relationship but your partner is still unsure, there is more advice in another book in this series: *Help Your Partner Say 'Yes'*.

How to End a Relationship and Mean It

One of the hardest ways to finish a relationship is what I call the 'stuttering end'. Instead of one clean break, the couple will give their relationship a second try and then a third. In the worst cases, I've met couples who have spent several years splitting and reconciling again. With each false dawn, the promises that it will be better this time are more extravagant, the disappointment more fundamental and the bitterness greater. Not only is the final end more painful but the recovery time is much longer. So what causes the stuttering end?

The problem is that the person instigating the break-up doesn't really mean it. In some cases, the instigator hopes that the drama of a threatened end will 'wake up' the other person but this is a high-risk strategy. It is much better to work on the specific issue – for example, we don't spend enough time together.

However, the main cause of the stuttering end is that the instigator gives a mixed message. For example: 'Although I don't love you any more, I don't hate you and maybe we could have a future in two, five, even ten years' time.' Most people would read this as goodbye, but someone desperate – especially if under the spell of limerence – will discount the negatives and build up the positives. Obviously, the instigator does not want to destroy their partner but letting the other person down gently can backfire. For example: 'You will always have a place in my heart.' It might be true, but someone under limerence will read this as: 'I don't really want to break up.' So how do you avoid the stuttering end?

1. **Don't ignore problems.** This is useful advice for any relationship – even happy ones. It is better to address issues as they happen rather than closing your eyes and hoping things will magically change.

2. **Be realistic about the prospects of fixing your relationship.** Although I have helped many

couples fall back in love again, they have generally been together for five years plus and have a basic foundation of good times to fall back on to. The extreme stuttering end couples, who have spent years in on–off relationships, generally have nothing in the 'happiness bank' beyond a burst of intense limerence at the very beginning.

3. **Have a good break-up.** Split up face to face and with enough time for the other person to ask questions or try and change your mind. It might seem easier to break up remotely – by email or on the phone – but the other person will feel cheated and pressure you into meeting up. Out of guilt, because it is not fair to split up at a distance, you will probably back down. However, you might have unwittingly set a pattern where your ex-partner uses guilt to force a series of concessions or even reconciliations.

4. **Give a clear message.** Stick to the facts and be careful not to offer false hopes like 'maybe' or 'some day' or 'in the future'.

5. **Accept that your ex-partner will be angry and hurt.** He or she will probably heap all the blame on you but trying to justify yourself only prolongs the agony. One of the

advantages of a break-up is that you no longer have to worry about what your partner thinks.

6. **Stick to your guns.** You might miss him or her but keep your doubts to yourself. Don't call and say: 'I was thinking of you and thought I'd find out how you were doing.'

7. **Remain polite but distant.** Respond with a simple note to flowers and presents but keep focused on your message: it's over. If she phones, keep it short and sweet: 'Sorry, I can't talk now.' If he emails to ask what you have been up to, reply with the bare minimum: 'Shopping with my mum, you know, same old stuff.' Your ex-partner might be a pain but anger and rows can provide enough drama to sustain someone who sees themselves as the tragically discarded lover.

8. **How realistic are the promises of change?** It is easy to promise to 'try harder' or to have a complete personality transformation but much harder to pull it off.

9. **Are you looking back with rose-tinted glasses or thinking 'If only . . .'?** Of course, your relationship would have been easier 'If only he did not live five hundred miles away' or 'If only she did not adore her family but they will

have nothing to do with me.' What are the chances of things changing?

10. **You can become friends but not just yet.** It is fine to aspire to being friends with your ex – they could even introduce you to someone special – but allow enough time to lapse for one type of relationship to end and for the other to begin. In the meantime, an invitation to your birthday party would be a mixed message. It might seem cruel but it is in everybody's best interests.

There is more help from another book in this series: *Heal and Move On*.

Summing Up

If you and your partner agree about the future, it is relatively easy to move forward. If your partner is ambivalent, try explaining your decision and the underlying thinking. Listen to your partner's response, without interrupting or trying to 'sell' your solution, and a way forward will slowly emerge. The problem comes when you have opposite opinions about the future. This is painful but at least everything that was previously hidden is now up for discussion and can finally be faced.

IN A NUTSHELL:

- Make certain that you are giving a consistent message to your partner.
- Don't put extra pressure on your partner and yourself by moving straight from talk to action. Allow a few days to let the decision sink in.
- Being honest with each other might be difficult but, ultimately, it is better than being stuck in limbo.

FINAL NUTSHELLS

1. Take Stock

Being stuck in limbo is bad for your relationship and undermines your self-confidence:

- Before deciding whether to stay and fight for your relationship or leave with good grace, look at your underlying attitudes and whether they are clouding your thinking.
- Are you confusing good sex with love, holding out for a soul partner or expecting to 'just know' if someone is right?
- Be reassured that you are not alone in finding it hard to decide; modern life and increased choice are making us more likely to be dissatisfied and worried that something better was amongst the discarded options.

Checkpoint: Make a commitment to change. Look at the following five questions: Have you convinced yourself you were in love when it was really lust? Have you had a relationship that was wrong for you but only accepted the truth months or even years after it finished? Have you mistaken tension and drama for love? Have you questioned a healthy relationship because you didn't feel head over heels in love *all* the time? Have you felt powerful chemistry and assumed it must be love?

If you answered yes to any one of these questions, promise yourself that you will avoid these unhelpful myths in the future.

2. Look at Your Partner

Love is not enough on its own for a relationship – you also need to be compatible:

- Have you believed that true love will conquer all and therefore ignored potentially fatal flaws in either your partner (such as being overly possessive, refusing to talk about problems or having a terrible temper) or your circumstances (such as conflicting religions, living long distances away, toxic stepchildren or your partner being still enmeshed with his or her ex-spouse)?

- Have you confused sympathy with love or put a higher premium on your partner's willingness to commit than overall compatibility?
- Does your partner put you down or deliberately undermine your self-esteem?
- Have you expected too much from your partner and are angry because he or she has not met some need – even though you have not or cannot properly explain it?

Checkpoint: Watch the movie of your relationship. Close your eyes and think back to when you first met, picture everything happening and listen to what is being said. Every time your partner says or does anything that makes you uncomfortable or anxious, open your eyes and write it down. Afterwards, go back to the movie and keep watching until the next problem. When you've finished, go back over your notes. What warning signs did you ignore? How does this more balanced picture of your relationship change things?

3. Look at Yourself

We learn about relationships by watching how our parents argue, fall out and, hopefully, make up. Until we are old enough to go to school, and discover other possibilities, we imagine our family's way is the only option. Therefore our parents' relationship becomes the template for our own or something that we consciously react against:

- Have you tended to choose people who are like your father or your mother? Maybe you've gone for lovers who seem different at the start but later you realise behave in similar ways?
- When looking back at recent relationships, have you played the same role – for example: rescuing your partner or being rescued; punishing your partner or soaking up his or her attacks; using controlling behaviour or being controlled?
- What links can you make between today and the past? To what extent are the issues between you and your partner a reflection of those witnessed when you were a child?
- Until we make peace with the past, we are doomed to repeat it.

Checkpoint: Do the fifty/fifty test. Instead of blaming your partner or taking all the blame yourself, find a balanced approach by dividing a piece of paper down the middle. On one side put all your partner's contributions to the problem and on the other put your own. Keep going until both sides have as many items as possible. If you can't find much for your side, look at how doing nothing contributed: 'I allowed him to take charge' or 'I opted out of family decisions and let her make all the decisions.' Generally, most problems are fifty/fifty. Finally, look at the items on your side of the divide: what changes would you like to make?

4. Understanding Intimacy

Without commitment, there is ultimately no relationship. So understanding if either you or your partner is frightened of commitment is vital for establishing the health of your relationship:

- Could your quest for the elusive someone who ticks all the boxes actually be a way of avoiding commitment?
- As the wit and author Quentin Crisp (1908–1999) said: 'There is no great dark man.'

However, there are lots of good people with whom we can rub along very nicely, and in the process lose some of our, and their, rough edges.

- So don't mistake the momentary discomfort of growing together as a fundamental flaw.
- If you consistently commit to inappropriate or unavailable people, understanding the pattern is the first step to making better choices in the future.

Checkpoint: What happens if you change your steps in the intimacy dance? If you tend to pull away from commitment, what happens if you take a step closer and, for example, stay until supper on Sunday night rather than leave after lunch? You might fear that your partner will overwhelm you with further demands for intimacy but what actually happens? If you are responsible for all the closeness, step back and let your partner make the moves. You might fear that he or she will drift further away but give it some time – like a couple of weeks – and your partner will probably take up the slack.

5. Get the Timing Right

Although we'd like to think that problems ignored will somehow get better of their own accord, unfortunately, they normally grow bigger and multiply:

- The best time to face a problem is now.
- Even if it is not possible to find a solution straight away, putting all the issues on the table will take the edge off a crisis.
- Remove the ticking clock. In most cases, there is no immediate hurry.
- Good decisions are seldom made under pressure.
- What splits up most couples is not the size of the problem but a feeling that one partner is not prepared to face up to it.

Checkpoint: Break the problem down into smaller parts. By taking small steps, you will sail calmly past obstacles that previously frightened or defeated you. Even better, it creates an appetite for more change and continuous success. So, for example, instead of worrying about how you'll deal with an empty house after years of bringing up children, focus on organising the perfect weekend away together.

6. Decision Time

You should be ready to move forward but if you are still stuck, look at what's holding you back.

- 'If only' thinking. This is when you are over-loaded with regrets: 'If only I'd not made that call' or 'If only we hadn't lost that baby'.
- While you are thinking about possible imaginary pasts, you are not living in the present with all its real possibilities.
- Some people are held back by guilt and fear of hurting their partner, their friends or their children.
- Instead of suppressing your feelings, look guilt full in the face. Have you exaggerated the effect on someone else? Have you taken more than your share of responsibility? With a more balanced understanding, think about how you could make amends or mitigate the impact of your decision.

Checkpoint: Identify the gifts and lessons. Out of every experience – however terrible – comes something positive. Perhaps you've learned not to be so trusting, the depth of your courage or the strength of a friendship. Maybe you've discovered a new passion for life or the value of forgiveness. Appreciating these lessons will help you step into the future without regrets.

7. Turning Your Decision into a Reality

Coming out of limbo can present a new set of problems:

- There is often a burst of adrenaline from getting off the fence and making a decision.
- This high can make you insensitive to the feelings of your partner.
- Be patient and explain all the thinking behind your decision.
- If you have decided to end your relationship, it is likely that your partner will be shocked or go into denial. He or she has not spent the last months examining every corner of your relationship, like you have, and will need time to catch up.
- If you want to commit but your partner disagrees, give yourself time to recover. Leaping into another relationship, without mourning the loss of this one, will cast a shadow over

subsequent relationships and undermine your recovery.

Checkpoint: Deal with the stress. Whatever your decision and the reaction of your partner, there will be wobbly moments. At these times, try this simple breathing exercise. It can be done sitting down with your eyes closed or walking down the street. As you breath in, say to yourself 'Yes'. Hold your breath for a second, be aware of your expanded lungs, and say 'I'. Finally, let your breath out slowly as you say 'can'. Repeating 'Yes I can' and following this simple breathing exercise – at least ten times in a row – will not only be calming but also keep you resolute.

FINAL NUTSHELL:

- People are often in limbo because they are frightened about the future.
- Come at the problem from a different angle and ask yourself different questions.
- There is no rush. Give yourself plenty of time to make an informed decision.

A Note on the Author

Andrew G. Marshall is a marital therapist and the author of *I Love You But I'm Not In Love With You: Seven Steps to Saving Your Relationship*, *The Single Trap: The Two-step Guide to Escaping It and Finding Lasting Love* and *How Can I Ever Trust You Again?: Infidelity: From Discovery to Recovery in Seven Steps*. He writes for *The Times*, the *Mail on Sunday*, the *Guardian*, *Psychologies* and women's magazines around the world. His work has been translated into over fifteen languages. Andrew trained with RELATE and has a private practice offering counselling, workshops, training days and inspirational talks.

www.andrewgmarshall.com

THE SEVEN STEPS SERIES

ARE YOU RIGHT FOR ME?
Seven steps to getting clarity and commitment in your relationship
ISBN 9781408802625 · PAPERBACK · £6.99

✳

HELP YOUR PARTNER SAY 'YES'
Seven steps to achieving better cooperation and communication
ISBN 9781408802632 · PAPERBACK · £6.99

✳

LEARN TO LOVE YOURSELF ENOUGH
Seven steps to improving your self-esteem and your relationships
ISBN 9781408802618 · PAPERBACK · £6.99

✳

RESOLVE YOUR DIFFERENCES
Seven steps to coping with conflict in your relationship
ISBN 9781408802595 · PAPERBACK · £6.99

✳

BUILD A LIFE-LONG LOVE AFFAIR
Seven steps to revitalising your relationship
ISBN 9781408802557 · PAPERBACK · £6.99

✳

HEAL AND MOVE ON
Seven steps to recovering from a break-up
ISBN 9781408802601 · PAPERBACK · £6.99

ORDER YOUR COPY:

BY PHONE: +44 (0)1256 302 699;

BY EMAIL: DIRECT@MACMILLAN.CO.UK

ONLINE: WWW.BLOOMSBURY.COM/BOOKSHOP

WWW.BLOOMSBURY.COM

BLOOMSBURY